NORTH CAROLINA
STATE BOARD OF COMMUNITY COLL
LIBRARIES
STANLY COMMUNITY COLLEGE

ETHICAL ARGUMENT

ETHICAL ARGUMENT

Critical Thinking in Ethics

HUGH MERCER CURTLER

[I]n subjects such as philosophy and literature, in which it is . . . respectable to entertain different opinions, teachers hesitate to teach their students how to choose among them, and hesitate themselves to choose.

But thought is applied to action through decision. Giving students ideas without enabling them to draw conclusions is like giving them sharpened tools without teaching them what to do with them.

RALPH BARTON PERRY

PARAGON HOUSE

New York

First edition, 1993

Published in the United States by

Paragon House Publishers
90 Fifth Avenue
New York, NY 10011

Copyright © 1993 by Paragon House

All rights reserved. No part of this book may be
reproduced, in any form, without written permission from
the publishers, unless by a reviewer who wishes
to quote brief passages.

Library of Congress Cataloging-in-Publication Data

Curtler, Hugh Mercer.
Ethical argument : critical thinking in ethics / Hugh Mercer
Curtler.—1st ed.
p.   cm.
Includes index.
ISBN 1-55778-513-9
1. Ethics.   2. Critical thinking.   3. Decision-making (Ethics)
I. Title.
BJ1012.C87   1993
170—dc20   91-44764
                                                        CIP

Manufactured in the United States of America

CONTENTS

v

ACKNOWLEDGMENTS

I would like to thank my colleague Stewart Day for reading several sections of an early draft and making several helpful suggestions. Former students, Kevin Stroup and Jill Anderson, read an early draft of the manuscript and made useful suggestions as well. I would especially like to thank Professors Kriste Taylor and Wallace Beasley for reading the manuscript in its entirety and making numerous helpful suggestions that resulted in a much improved text.

And finally, I would like to thank my wife Linda who put up with a preoccupied husband for months on end and then read the manuscript with great care to make certain that the ideas were expressed in the clearest possible manner.

Several of the thirty-seven case studies in Chapter Six are from a "Report of the Committee for Education in Business Ethics" sponsored by a grant from the National Endowment for the Humanities in 1980. I thank Norman Bowie for permission to use those cases. While most of the remainder of the case studies are original, several have been borrowed from Michael Bayles' book *Professional Ethics* © 1981 by Wadsworth, Inc. They are printed by permission of the publisher. The DOONESBURY cartoons © Gary Trudeau in 1984, 1985, 1986, and 1987 are used by permission of Universal Press Syndicate, as are the CALVIN AND HOBBES cartoons, © 1989 Universal Press Syndicate.

PREFACE

This book is written for the undergraduate student who has had little or no previous philosophy. It seeks to bridge the gap between theory and practice in ethics. Centering around a critique of ethical relativism, together with a defense of objectivism, the book takes a firm stand on a number of controversial issues, a novel feature in an introductory text. The view that respect for persons is an inviolable principle, for example, together with the attempt to combine deontology with rule utilitarianism, are not positions that are widely shared. Neither is the "ethical perspective" from which ethically irrelevant practical and motivational considerations, such as short-run self-interest, are excluded. These views are adopted in this book, for the most part, in order to generate discussion.

Following an examination of basic ethical theory, and after strategies and procedures have been devised, the student is shown how to apply ethical principles to conflict, how to distinguish good ethical reasons from rationalization, and how to recognize good ethical reasons generally. By speaking directly to the student (without insulting his or her intelligence), by avoiding technical jargon as much as possible, and by the use of numerous examples and cartoons, the book seeks to draw the student automatically into the activity of doing philosophy. Emphasis, therefore, is on process and the acquisition of transferable skills rather than on content as such. At the same time, every effort has been made to cover the issues that are fundamental to any introductory ethics course.

The book is designed to be used as a "core text" for courses in general ethics, medical, legal, business, or professional ethics, and for courses in critical thinking. The text can be supplemented by primary source material, additional cases in the area(s) of major concern, or more extensive work in logic.

INTRODUCTION: TO THE STUDENT

By presenting a series of arguments that are designed to persuade the reader that ethics is a suitable arena for rational deliberation, this book seeks to refute relativism in ethics. The arguments will show that ethics is not just an arena for conflicting personal opinions and differing cultural perspectives, as is popularly believed.

We will adopt the Socratic method that stresses the need for criticism as a *positive* means to more reliable conclusions. This method was called *maieutic* by the Greeks. It involves careful scrutiny of truth claims and the rejection of those claims that cannot withstand criticism. The remaining claims can be considered "true" unless or until further criticism dislodges them. This is not to say that truth can be *defined* in terms of non-falsehood; a claim is not true just because it cannot be shown to be false. That would mean that if the claim "Caesar had freckles" cannot be shown to be false it must be true. But the same thing could be said about the claim "Caesar did not have freckles," and this would be absurd. Something cannot be both true and false at the same time and in the same respect. What we are saying is that a claim can be *considered* true if we cannot show it to be false. It is true *so far as we know at present*. In ethics this is often the best we can do, but it is considerably better than simply saying that truth and falsehood have no place in ethical conflict.

One way of looking at the critical examination of ethical claims and counter-claims is to imagine ourselves at a trial as jury members who know that a crime has been committed but don't know who did it. We must listen to the evidence and weigh it carefully before reaching a conclusion "beyond a reasonable doubt" as to the identity of the guilty party. The main problem with this analogy is that ethical claims like "Sally *shouldn't have* murdered the milk-man for leaving whole milk instead of skim" are different from factual claims like "Sally murdered the milkman for leaving whole milk instead of skim." Some say the differences are so important that any attempt to liken ethical investigation to determinations of matters of fact—as in the case of a jury trial in which there clearly is a guilty party—is bogus: ethics is about personal feelings, not about facts. These critics insist that ethical claims are not "truth claims," or claims that purport to be true; they are simply state-ments about how we feel about things that happen—I get upset when I think about Sally's having murdered the milkman, and that's why I say it was wrong.

This criticism would reduce ethics to a purely subjective, or personal, level, and is firmly rejected in this book. So also is the related view that would reduce ethical claims to statements about shared feelings and attitudes in a given culture or subculture. Clearly, there are feelings involved in ethics, and certainly it is the case that our ethical pronouncements frequently reflect those feel-ings. It may even be the case that occasionally our ethical judg-ments are nothing more than an expression of our feelings or the feelings of those among whom we live. But it does not follow from any of these statements that ethical judgments can be *reduced* to those feelings in all cases. That is to say, we can admit that subjec-tive factors enter into ethical judgments without allowing that there is nothing else involved. There may be excellent support for the claim made above that Sally shouldn't have murdered the milkman—aside from the fact that thinking about it upsets us. Before we decide that the ethical claim is just a "matter of opin-ion," or a mere expression of feeling, we need to see whether or not there is any support for it, and, if there is, to examine that support. *The question of whether ethical claims are "subjective" or "objective" is decided on the grounds of the support (or lack of support) for those claims, rather than on the claims themselves.* Rational support for our ethical claims comprises what we call "justification." The objectivity of ethical judgments, then, is a function of justification: to the extent that we can justify ethical judgments, they are objec-tive.

One of our chief concerns in ethical argument, then, is to see if we can find evidence and argument support for the claims we make in ethics. If that support is strong, and if it is not culture-bound, then anyone at any time should follow the argument and accept the claim that comprises the argument's conclusion. If the claim commands our consent because of the compelling nature of the support for that claim, then we can say with some confidence that the claim is not simply a matter of personal opinion or cultural perspective: it is "objective." As the contemporary British philosopher Karl Popper has said, "objective means *justifiable*, independently of anybody's whim: a justification is 'objective' if in principle it can be tested and understood by anybody."[1] Whether or not I *want* to accept a reasonable conclusion, I *must*, if I am honest and capable of following the argument. What we seek in ethics are precisely those elements and features of an ethical argument that we are compelled to accept whether we want to or not, "independently of anybody's whim."

Much of what is discussed in this book will be centered around the question of justification in ethics. Since justification is a matter of evidence and argument support, we will want to know what makes arguments strong or weak, how to forge strong ethical arguments, and how to dismantle weak ethical arguments. We will want to know what constitute "good ethical reasons" in support of ethical arguments and how to weigh reasons, pro and con, to reach reasonable ethical decisions.

The success of our attempt to refute ethical relativism will depend on whether or not we can make our case on behalf of sound reasoning in ethics. We shall see whether or not strong arguments provide escape from the morass of conflicting opinions and feelings that, for many people, seem to be the whole of ethics. We do not contend that ethical claims can be made with certainty, or that any one of us is in the privileged position of having "The Truth" in ethics. But we reject the position of the relativist that would leave us with no reasonable way to resolve ethical conflict and no sensible way to make ethical decisions. We seek a middle ground, acknowledging the uncertainty that surrounds ethics without giving in to the temptation to throw up our hands and conclude that the uncertainty is ineradicable.

As I say this I imply an assumption that must be made explicit. I assume that "reasonable" approaches to ethical conflict are prefer-able to "unreasonable" ones. In speaking about "reasonableness" I follow the contemporary American philosopher Brand Blanshard who said that

> By reasonableness I do not mean intelligence, though that may be a great help. Attila, Torquemada, and Stalin were highly intelligent men, but they were not reasonable men. Nor is a reasonable man necessarily a learned man, for learning may be present without even ordinary common sense. No; the reasonableness of which I am speaking is a settled disposition to guide one's belief and conduct by the evidence. It is a bent of the will to order one's thoughts by the relevant facts, to order one's practice in the light of the values involved, to make reflective judgment the compass of one's belief and action.[2]

Whether or not readers find this plea for reasonableness and its attendant rejection of relativism convincing, they should at least suspend judgment until they have carefully considered the argu-ments presented in these pages. The ultimate goal of this book is to encourage readers to engage in ethical reasoning by means of a critical examination of the book's central argument.

Is it possible to liken ethical reasoning to a jury trial in which someone is truly guilty or innocent? That is, is there anything like a fact at the center of ethical conflict to which we must consent because of the nature of the evidence for that fact? Or is ethics reducible to a jumble of personal opinions, none of which is any "better" than the others? These are the central questions that confront us as we begin our examination of ethical argument.

PLAN OF THE WORK

After a brief dialogue between Rick and Nina, two imaginary students who worry about whether or not people in one culture are ever in a position to make value judgments about activities that take place in another culture, the book begins with a careful dis-cussion of ethical relativism. The view is defined and criticized in Section One of Chapter One, and the counter thesis, namely, that

ethical judgments when carefully grounded in evidence and argument are not relative to persons or cultures, is defended. In the
third section of Chapter One, we try to determine the limits to
which we can claim that ethical judgments are non-relative, or
objective. It is suggested that in ethics, as in the case of history and
even the exact sciences, subjective or personal elements enter into
our judgments, but we need not allow that ethical judgments (any
more than historical or scientific judgments) can be *reduced* to
those personal elements.

In Chapter Two we examine several ethical principles that will
provide a framework for the discussion in the remainder of the
book, as they have in ethics generally for many years. We propose
that respect for persons be regarded as fundamental in ethics together with fairness. Further, we add the admonition to adopt a
rule that will maximize human happiness (consistent with respect
for persons and fairness) in order to adopt ethical options and
resolve ethical conflicts. This discussion gives rise to an examination of "The Ethical Perspective" from which we can see more
clearly how such conflicts are to be resolved and such choices
made. The ethical perspective requires that we ignore short-run
self-interest and practical considerations (for a time); we must seek
a perspective that is disinterested and cognizant of the long term,
and allows us to imagine ourselves in the place of the victims of
iniquity.

After a brief "interlude" to look in on our imaginary students,
Rick and Nina, we begin to forge the tools of ethical argument in
Chapter Three. We examine the structure of arguments and the
factors that contribute to strength or weakness in those arguments.
The second section of Chapter Three presents four of the most
common informal fallacies that we should be aware of in trying to
structure sound ethical arguments and reject weak ones.

The heart of the text lies in Chapter Four in which we examine in
considerable detail the process of justification in ethics. Justification is contrasted with rationalization and explanation and provides the grounds for claiming objectivity in ethics. Those ethical
claims are objective that we can support with evidence and argument in a way that can withstand criticism and appeal to a neutral
audience . . . such as a jury in a crime trial. This is the focus of the
fourth chapter and of the text as a whole.

In Chapter Five four case studies are presented in some detail as students are given an idea how to approach ethical conflicts critically and how to put together sound arguments of their own.

The final chapter provides thirty-seven cases in a variety of subject areas, from sports to medicine, for discussion and analysis.

PRELUDE: SETTING THE STAGE

In order to get our discussion under way, consider the following imaginary conversation between two students who have just left a philosophy class not unlike the one you are taking.

NINA: I think apartheid is wrong.

RICK: You mean as it is practiced in South Africa?

NINA: Exactly. I think it's wrong for one group of people—no matter how large or small—to exploit another group for any reason, and especially for reasons of economics.

RICK: Don't you think that's for the South Africans to decide?

NINA: What do you mean?

RICK: Well, it's a bit presumptuous of you, an American, to make judgments about another culture when all you know about that culture is what you've heard or read in the newspapers. You've never even visited that country, much less lived there. You can't possibly know what reasons the South Africans have for their cultural attitudes and convictions . . . and that includes apartheid. You only know what is written in American newspapers and magazines and that's full of bias. What right do you have to say what the people in South Africa should and should not do?

NINA: It's not really a question of "rights" is it? I mean, don't we have a *responsibility* to speak up when something is wrong—in our own culture or any other culture for that matter?

RICK: I don't think so. Not at all. It's like the rules of a game. The white people of South Africa, being of Dutch descent, like to play rugby in their spare time. We like to play football. Who's to say we're right and they're wrong? They speak with a different accent, too, and they probably dress differently. Can we say those sorts of things are wrong, too, just because they're different?

NINA: Well. . . .

RICK: Let me give you a different example. When the U.S. invaded Panama and overthrew Manuel Noriega, the military leaders of the U.S. Army insisted that the Panamanians keep a strong military presence "to provide security for the Panama Canal." The people of Panama themselves wanted no army at all, or at most a very weak military presence, because they had been under strong military rule for twenty years and they wanted no more of it. Now I ask you: what right do we have to tell them what's good for them?

NINA: Wait a minute! Don't go so fast! You are confusing three things: apartheid, games, and the advice of our military people to Panama. I would agree with much of what you say about games, and insofar as no one gets hurt, many of the customs and practices of other countries are like games. The example of the army in Panama is more like a game than is apartheid, because it's more a question of tactics than anything else and presumably no one gets hurt. Apartheid, on the other hand, could very well require intervention in order to prevent harm to others and to help preserve the rights of the blacks in that country. I would agree that involvement in another country's self-determination is always wrong unless there are compelling ethical reasons. But I'm not advocating intervention here; I'm simply saying they are wrong. I'm making an ethical judgment, and you're saying I have no "right" to do that. I say that when people's rights are being violated that is grounds for ethical condemnation. It's possible that intervention is also called for, but that's another matter entirely.

RICK: But what you call "rights" are not recognized by the white people of South Africa, as far as we know. You want to impose your ethical views on them.

NINA: Only if my ethical views are *correct*.

RICK: But how can you know that? There is no such thing as a "correct" ethical view! There are only my ethical views, yours, and the South Africans, in this case. There are clearly differences among them, but none is any more "correct" than the others. It's all relative.

NINA: Relative to what? To culture?

RICK: Yes, for the most part. We are all products of what anthropologists call "enculturation" and we take in attitudes and beliefs with our mother's milk. We aren't even aware of what those attitudes and beliefs are half the time! We certainly don't question them; we assume them and in the end we fall back on them because they seem self-evident. All your fancy talk about "rights" is simply a thinly disguised verbal camouflage for what is nothing more or less than a cultural prejudice.

NINA: You are saying that the concept of human rights is nothing more than a cultural prejudice?

RICK: Yes, if you must.

NINA: But a prejudice is something that precedes judgment and excludes reasons. On the other hand, the claim that humans have rights is one that I can support with reasons that *anyone* should accept, not just those in my culture. Clearly there is a difference between these claims and others that cannot be supported by reasons and that do not withstand criticism— claims that clearly *are* nothing more than bias in this or any other culture. Your view collapses all claims to the same level as bias or prejudice. That's ridiculous! You're throwing the baby out with the bath water!

RICK: I'm not sure what you mean. Give me an example.

NINA: Let's suppose I'm a teacher and you are a student.

RICK: OK. I'll go along with that. But I think you've got it backwards!

NINA: Anyway, as a teacher I belong to what is, technically, a subculture of a culture we'll call "Academia." We'll call that subculture "T."

RICK: Agreed.

NINA: And in my culture there is another subculture "S" made up of students just like you.

RICK: OK.

NINA: Members of my subculture agree that henceforth we will all evaluate the work of our students in the following fashion:

those sitting closest to the front of the room will receive A's and those sitting closest to the back of the room will receive F's and those sitting in between will receive corresponding grades.

RICK: You mean, those sitting in the second row will get B's and third row C's and so forth?

NINA: Yes.

RICK: No way! That's ridiculous! It's totally unfair.

NINA: Why do you say that? Members of my subculture have agreed on this procedure, and if the students don't like it they can leave and go someplace else where things are done "fairly."

RICK: But your group's determinations are arbitrary and capricious. Anyone can see that!

NINA: That's *your* opinion. But don't forget you're not in my culture. What right do you have to say we're not being fair?

RICK: *Anyone* can see it's not fair! Grades in your system would no longer represent anything meaningful; there would be no relation whatever between the grade and performance. Knowledge would count for nothing. Students wouldn't be motivated to learn anything; they would simply fight for seats in the front row. That's an absurd example!

NINA: Is it? Or is it just like apartheid? Aren't the students in subculture "S" just like the blacks in South Africa? At least, aren't they like them in important respects? Aren't you getting all upset here because the example involves people like *you* and you can identify with them? The reasons you gave (that my grading system is arbitrary and capricious) are reasons you think *anyone* in any culture should accept! Isn't that so? And you're right! Those are good reasons in that they are binding on people in my subculture as well as those in your subculture. They certainly aren't disguised prejudices as you said earlier: they have nothing to do with culture.

RICK: But they do, in a way. My subculture recognizes these reasons, whereas yours does not.

NINA: Yes, but my subculture *should* recognize these reasons, don't you think? Indeed, my subculture should recognize *any* truth claim that is supported by reasons, in ethics or anywhere else for that matter. If people in my subculture insist that our grading system is fair after they have heard your arguments against it they're a bit like the members of the Flat Earth Society, who insist that the earth is flat even though the evidence doesn't support that claim. Your reasons for rejecting our grading system are like the reasons given in the sciences against the flat earth hypothesis: their appeal cuts across cultures. The appeal is in some sense universal. Anyone who follows the argument and weighs the evidence *should* accept the conclusion.

RICK: Perhaps so. But they won't, and you know it.

NINA: You're right. I do know it. But that's beside the point. It's for the psychologists to tell us why it is that people don't accept as true those things for which there are strong reasons. Why do people continue to believe that the earth is flat? I don't know. Do you? That's not our problem.

RICK: Yes, but I still think the strength of those reasons is a cultural phenomenon. Strong reasons in one culture will seem weak in another culture. To go back to our original example, what possible meaning does the phrase "human rights" have to a group of people for whom blacks are not even human?

NINA: Ah yes, but that's a question that can easily be settled by the biologist. That's a fairly easy matter, and like many of the reasons that support ethical claims, it's a matter of fact. The easiest way to handle the question is to examine the supposed reasons that support the claim that blacks are not human. We see whether these "reasons" can stand up to criticism; that's how we proceed: propose and dispose. Examine the evidence, sift through it, and accept only those reasons and that evidence that can withstand criticism. This is not a cultural matter; it is a matter for any reasonable person. Good reasons are culture blind.

RICK: Perhaps so, and perhaps not. Surely cultural bias enters in. There's no way to avoid it at some point in the argument. Aren't you likely to consider *anyone* who disagrees with you as "unreasonable"? Isn't your position likely to lead to intolerance, an unwillingness to consider any position that conflicts with your own "reasonable" position?

NINA: That's a possibility, of course. But that's the point of the method of proposal and disposal: it's supposed to be used to examine *my* convictions as well as those of others who disagree with me. It may well be that I am being the unreasonable one. It doesn't have to be the other person. Personal and cultural bias can crop up anywhere, and it is important that we keep an open mind and eliminate it anywhere we find it. We may never be entirely rid of it, but criticism will help us get rid of much of it, and more each time we reconsider our arguments, we would hope.

RICK: Then what you're saying is that the "truth" of ethical claims is a matter of more or less, not either/or? It is a matter of strong reasons, or good reasons, which are always more or less infected with cultural bias. Is that it?

NINA: I think so. But I'm not sure I know what you mean by truth being a matter of "more or less" and not "either/or."

RICK: Well, you know. In math, for example, the statement $2+2=4$ is either true or it's false. There's no middle ground. In history, on the other hand, statements like "The Persians assisted the Spartans in their war against the Athenians in the fifth century B.C." are more or less true (or probable)—depending on the weight of the evidence. Or in psychology, if we say that "a person who lives in a densely populated area is more likely to become violent than if the same person lived in a rural area" that statement is more or less probable, again, depending on the weight of the evidence. What you're saying is that ethical claims are more like the claims in history and psychology than they are like the claims in mathematics. Right?

NINA: Yes. That's it.

* * *

As the title of the section you have just read suggests, this dialogue sets the stage for the remainder of the book. A great many students who come to ethics for the first time tend to take Rick's position, pretty much as we have presented it here—though they might not give in quite so easily to Nina's arguments! For that reason, I will try to persuade you that Nina espouses the stronger position. You may or may not agree, but one of the rules of the game is that you must try to see both sides of the issue as you proceed and keep an open mind. Whether or not you come to agree with Nina in the end, you will have done some serious thinking about ethical issues and ethical points of view—and that's what is most important!

CHAPTER ONE

IS IT ALL A MATTER OF OPINION?

Relativism Versus Objectivism

1. CLAIMS IN ETHICS: A CRITIQUE OF RELATIVISM

Historians of science tell us that relativism began to permeate Western thought in the late nineteenth century. At that time non-euclidian geometry had begun to challenge the classical view "that all knowledge was unitary. If one found a kind of certainty in geometry, then one could hope for the same kind of certainty in physics, in biology, in ethics, or in religion."[1] In conjunction with non-euclidian geometry, Darwinism, scientific naturalism, and the new sociology and anthropology made it possible by 1900 for William Graham Sumner to state categorically that "there is no natural law; there are no natural rights, and there is nothing *a priori*. The only natural right is the right to struggle for survival."[2]

Astonishingly, relativism has become so prevalent in our day that it is not restricted to value judgments, but includes other types of judgments as well, including perceptual judgments. As N. L. Gifford tells us:

Naive relativism is certainly alive and well in the idioms of our ordinary language. 'True for you, true for me' is echoed in 'to each

1

his own,' 'everyone is entitled to his own opinion,' 'when in Rome do as the Romans do,' 'different strokes for different folks,' and 'whatever feels good,' to cite but a few examples. We use these idioms casually and comfortably. There seems to be little need to ask ourselves what we are really saying. In fact, we might not even consider ourselves relativists when we use these expressions. . . . They become a familiar part of our environment. We can expect that just the repetition of such relativistic expressions *can* produce in the speakers of the language a predisposition to uncritically accept or prefer relativistic positions on the grounds of familiarity (sometimes called 'common sense').[3]

Relativism in Ethics

In ethics, at any rate, many people share Rick's view in the dialogue you read in the Prelude. For such people, ethical disputes are merely conflicts among various desires, wishes, interests, attitudes, and likes or dislikes—all of which are relative to the individuals involved in the disputes or, perhaps, to their respective cultures. Thus, according to such people, if I judge that the Hitler Youth were perverse in wanting to annihilate the Jews, or that the Iroquois were misguided when they tortured their enemies to determine the limits of their endurance to pain, that is merely my "opinion"—which is a collective term we use to include all or most of the words in the long list given above. According to the popular view, these "opinions" are not subject to rational argument beyond individual or cultural boundaries and, according to this view, ethics currently wallows in a subjective quagmire in which reason has no place. Surely, this is a mistaken view.

What Are Ethical Claims About?

The central issue in the relativism/nonrelativism issue is over the question of whether value judgments are about subjects and cultures or about events and objects in the world independent of those subjects and cultures. If I say "Brutus was wrong to have killed Caesar," am I saying something about myself (subjectivism), about my culture (cultural relativism), or about the event itself (nonrelativism, or objectivism)?

In the first case, the judgment either expresses my personal antipathy toward the event ("That kind of thing gives me the creeps") or else it states a claim about my attitude toward the event ("It is true that I disapprove of that sort of thing"). In the second case, the judgment makes a claim about the dominant attitude in my culture toward such events ("Generally speaking, such things are not acceptable in my culture: it is against the law"). In the third case, the judgment claims to be about the event itself—regardless of my likes and dislikes or those of the people in my culture ("It is wrong for Brutus to have killed Caesar"). *The determination of whether we are making the judgment from a relative or nonrelative stance depends on the kinds of reasons given for the claim in every case.*

For the subjectivist/relativist, the reasons support the claim that one does, in fact, disapprove of such events—or there are no reasons because there is no judgment, merely an expression of one's feelings about the event in question. For the cultural relativist, the reasons support the claim that persons generally, within a given culture, do, as a matter of fact, have (culturally accepted) reasons for disapproving of such things as killing. For the nonrelativist/objectivist, compelling reasons support the claim that the action was wrong and, therefore, anybody at any time should agree with those reasons and conclusions, regardless of personal or cultural predispositions.

The Truth of Ethical Claims

For the nonrelativist, value judgments such as "It was wrong for Brutus to have killed Caesar" cannot be both true and false: they are either true or they are false for the reasons given, or other reasons as yet to be determined. It is important to note, however, that the nonrelativist does *not* argue that he or she *knows* whether the claim is true, only that it is *either* true *or* false. For the nonrelativist, ethical claims resemble ordinary perceptual claims such as "the cat is on the mat," except that they are harder to verify.

For the relativist/subjectivist, on the other hand, value judgments can be *both* true and false—true for you (or your culture) but false for me (or my culture). The tricky thing is that the differences between relativism and nonrelativism cannot be determined by simply looking at or listening to the way the claims are expressed:

the claims all look alike! As mentioned above, the difference is found in the kinds of reasons given in each case. Thus, the question "why?" becomes pivotal in ethical reasoning. Let us look more closely:

A. Relativism/Subjectivism
"Brutus was wrong to have killed Caesar."

"Why?"

"Because I just feel that way. That sort of thing makes me sick. I can't stand violence. Yuk!!" etc. etc.

The claim is about the speaker, or writer, and is therefore subjective (relative to the subject).

B. Cultural Relativism
"Brutus was wrong to have killed Caesar."

"Why?"

"Because people in my culture don't do that sort of thing. It is illegal and/or morally repugnant to people like me."

The claim is about the speaker's culture (and himself or herself as a part of that culture) and is therefore culturally relative.

C. Nonrelativism/Objectivism
"Brutus was wrong to have killed Caesar."

"Why?"

"Because it violates ethical principles concerning respect for life, principles that are basic to any human society." (OR) "Brutus miscalculated the effects on Rome and the action produced the opposite effect from the one he intended and resulted in pain and suffering for a great many Romans. Thus, even if one tries to justify the action itself in terms of consequences, those consequences show that the action was wrong."

This is a nonrelative claim that is supported by reasons that are accessible to anybody at any time—regardless of one's personal or cultural bias.

The differences among the claims being made in these three cases must be determined by examining the reasons and evidence provided. We shall denote the difference by referring to "relative claims," and "nonrelative claims." In doing this, we shall consider subjectivism and cultural relativism to be two types of relativism and as systematically alike, even though the latter view is more plausible than the former and therefore needs to be taken more seriously. In any event, both views contrast sharply with non-relativism, or objectivism, which is the view we are defending here.

Ethical Claims and Perceptual Claims Compared

On the face of it, relativism—especially in its guise as subjectivism—is an absurd view. This is certainly true if the view is extended to include all judgments whatsoever. The notion that all judgments uttered by a person depend *for their truth* on that person is incredible. The relativist seems to have a loose hold on the rather obvious fact that Smith *says* that "A robin is larger than a wren" and infers incorrectly that therefore "A robin is larger than a wren for Smith (and no one else)." But there are clearly many judgments that are legitimate claims, open to verification or falsification by persons other than the one making the judgment. One would ordinarily hesitate to allow empirical judgments like "A robin is larger than a wren" to be dismissed as mere reflections on the convictions of the speaker. Such judgments seem to claim *something* about the world for which we are prepared to offer some evidence. Let us look at this difference carefully.

Any statement that makes a claim about the world "out there" and not simply about the person making the claim or about his or her feelings about that world, is claiming that the world is a certain way and that what he or she is saying about that world is true if and only if the world is the way that person says it is. That is, the claim points to an objective state of affairs, a state of affairs open to independent, third person, verification or falsification. Such a claim is, as we have said, a nonrelative claim and not merely a relative claim. It is one thing to say that "A robin is larger than a wren" and quite another to say "Smith believes that a robin is larger than a wren." It is also quite different from saying "robins are considered larger than wrens in Smith's culture." The latter statements are statements about the speaker, or the speaker's culture. Accordingly, they are verified or falsified by finding things out about the speaker or the speaker's culture. The former, however, is about our shared world and can be verified or falsified by finding things out about how the world happens to be—regardless of cultural perspective. The former is a *nonrelative claim*, a claim that professes to be true about our world, whereas the latter is simply a statement about the speaker or the speaker's culture.

Justification in Ethics as a Function of Support

If we are going to make good the claim that ethical judgments can sometimes be treated the way we treat ordinary nonrelative judgments of perception, we must establish what the eighteenth-century German philosopher Immanuel Kant referred to as "objective and sufficient" grounds for ethical judgments, grounds that make those judgments acceptable to anybody who considers them carefully and critically. In a word, we are seeking "justification" for our ethical judgments. For this justification to be nonrelative, the grounds or support for the claims that purport to constitute justification must be true for *anybody* who examines them critically. Rational criticism sometimes reveals the truth of our claims, but most often it reveals falsehood. After rejecting the false claims, we can regard the remainder as true—so far as we know at present. This is the key to Socratic *maieutic,* which is the method we shall adopt for ethical reasoning.

When we make objective claims, then, we can say they are true to the extent that (1) we can verify them or falsify them ourselves at another time, (2) someone *else* (regardless of that person's cultural biases) can verify or falsify those claims, and (3) the claims can withstand rational criticism. These three considerations result in the gradual elimination of subjective and cultural factors and the identification of those factors in our judgments that are objective, cross-cultural, and impersonal. The method is not perfect, but it can be quite successful. It involves proposal and disposal, criticism and defense, modification and adaptation. Above all else, it requires an open mind.

The subjective and relative factors in ethical claims usually take the form of ignorance, fear, superstition, bigotry, prejudice, emotional attachment, and bias, both personal and cultural. In ethics, sad to say, these factors can be predominant. Once we have recognized and, where possible, eliminated these personal and cultural factors, we then try to find reasons and evidence that will appeal to all persons of rational capacity and good will—regardless of the time and place in which those persons live.

Food for Further Thought

The thesis offered here is a difficult one to swallow, especially if one is in the habit of dismissing ethical or aesthetic judgments as mere "opinions." The notion that we can make judgments of the sort "Shakespeare was a great writer" and insist that this is a claim that can be verified rankles many people. They think it implies elitism, the view that we are saying we have superior knowledge, that we know things that others don't know. They ask: who's to say that Shakespeare was a *better* writer than, say, Micky Spillane? That's absurd! I love to read Micky Spillane and find Shakespeare totally boring. Indeed, how can we even say he was "great" when we don't know what that means?

These are good questions and they will recur in later chapters where we shall attempt to deal with them directly. For the moment we can only point out that there is no claim to superior knowledge implied in this position: no one presumes to *know* for sure what makes Shakespeare "great." The thesis here is that Shakespeare either is or is not great: he cannot be both. Whichever view is correct can be rationally defended by anyone who wants to take the time to determine what is distinctive about Shakespeare and what makes some writers better than others.

A philosophy instructor once made the statement in a class that Albert Schweitzer was a better man than Hitler. Now, aside from the fact that no one in that class knew who Albert Schweitzer was (a medical doctor and an organist of considerable talent and ability who turned his back on fame and fortune in Germany to treat poor natives in Africa), it appeared to the instructor that this was a statement everyone would accept. Not so! The students in the class were outraged that anyone would go so far as to say that one human being was better (or worse) than another. They noted that in a room full of skinhead neo-Nazis the claim would be roundly denounced, because all in the room would insist that Hitler was the better man. This objection is excellent and raises a good point: what do we do if some, or all, who weigh the "rational support" for the claims we make *reject* that support? This can happen: it probably would happen in a room full of neo-Nazis, just as a room full of members of the Flat Earth Society would deny that the earth is round. But it is fairly clear that such a room is full of people who are in principle incapable of weighing reasons and considering truth claims: they are blinded by their prejudices. But couldn't we say this about anyone who disagrees with us? Yes, we could, but in this case it does make some sense. Ask yourself: is there *any* argument a neo-Nazi would accept that would persuade him that Hitler was a bad man? One of the conditions that is necessary for rational deliberation to take place, the Socratic *maieutic* we mentioned earlier, is that we keep an open mind—at least as much as possible. That is why we attempt, as far as we can, to identify and remove those factors in ethical judgments and attempts at ethical justification that blind us to truth: prejudice and bias, what we have called the "subjective or cultural factors." None of us can do this completely (probably), but neo-Nazis cannot do this at all—at least not when it comes to the consideration of whether or not Hitler was a good or a bad man. We shall pursue the matter of prejudice in greater depth in the third section of this chapter.

The road ahead in this book is not easy. Ethical reasoning takes concentration and effort, as we have already seen. But if we begin with the conviction that it is impossible—the relativistic stance—we cannot even begin! So at the very least we should allow, at the outset, that it is *possible* to engage in ethical reasoning, to discover rational foundations for our ethical judgments. If after making the attempt we decide it cannot be done, then we shall be in a position to say so.

One important point should be noted in passing. It is much more *interesting* and more fruitful to insist that value judgments are objective claims than to succumb to the popular tendency to reduce them all to personal beliefs or opinions. The objectivist thesis defended in this book opens many doors to investigation that would otherwise remain closed. If a judgment isn't about our shared world, it holds no philosophical interest for the rest of us. It seems a mistake, however, to relegate all value judgments to the sphere of personal opinions. As N. L. Gifford so nicely puts it, "It is an unfortunate consequence of the curious relativistic positions that they ultimately encourage us to turn away from the larger world about which we are so curious."[4] One might go even further and call relativism a pernicious doctrine: it ends discussion before it can begin by insisting that there is no point, no possible outcome. If, on the other hand, we can treat value judgments as reasonable beliefs or objective claims about our common world then we can discuss them, agree or disagree about them, and settle disputes about them in a rational manner—at least some of the time.

2: THE CASE FOR OBJECTIVISM IN ETHICAL ARGUMENT

Asserting that ethical relativism is unacceptable and that ethical judgments can be reasonable claims and not disguised personal beliefs is one thing; making the case for this assertion is another.

To begin with, we need a better grasp of what it means to say that ethical judgments are, or can be, "objective," and a better understanding of how, as specifically ethical judgments, they resemble and differ from other types of judgments. Because of the obvious differences between ethical judgments and, for example, ordinary judgments of perception we tend to dismiss ethical judgments as merely "relative" while we allow that perceptual judgments are nonrelative or objective, and as such either true or false. Although the differences are certainly quite real, there are important similarities as well, and we need to attend to these to be fair in our assessment of ethical judgments.

In the last section, we spoke about Shakespeare's "greatness." Let's shift gears slightly and place our discussion in the framework of ethics. Our point will be the same, though we need to expand it somewhat. If I say "George is a good man" that is very different from saying "George is over six feet tall." I can see and measure height, but I cannot see or measure "goodness." Does it follow from this, though, that I have no reasonable grounds for making the *claim* that George is a good man? That is, can we provide no evidence for claims other than that provided by sensory experience—what can be seen and measured? Or is there more to verification and justification than mere sensation?

Possible Parallels with Science and the Social Sciences

Let us take three very different judgments, one from astronomy, one from history, and one from ethics, and let us see what constitutes verification, or justification, in each case. In doing so we should note the similarities as well as the differences; if we are to make the case that ethical claims are nonrelative claims, we must know how to verify claims we know to be nonrelative and see whether anything like that occurs in the case of ethical claims.

Our first example is from science and it states something none of us is likely to question:

(C1) "The earth encircles the sun annually in an elliptical orbit."

The second example is an historical claim:

(C2) Greece and Sumeria were closely linked during the late Bronze Age."

The third example is from ethics:

(C3) "Radar detectors should be outlawed."

Whether or not the third example is true is irrelevant for our present purposes. In saying that it is a "claim" we are simply saying that it *claims* to be true; that is, there is a procedure for testing it and for accepting or rejecting it as true or false based on the evidence that supports it. That is, it can be verified or falsified. To see how we might verify (justify) the third claim, we need to see how verification takes place in the more straightforward examples from science and history.

Scientific Claims

In the example from science (C1) we have a judgment that is not, strictly speaking, based on perception. The evidence that supports the claim is mostly from mathematics and physics. Much of the sensory evidence cannot be relied upon because it "cuts both ways": it can be used to support either the geocentric or the heliocentric hypotheses, as they are called. The sun's apparent movement can be accounted for either by the motion of the earth or by the motion of the sun. The mathematical evidence, however, is almost entirely on the side of the heliocentric hypothesis, suggested by the Polish astronomer Copernicus. Therefore his hypothesis can today lay claim to the title of "the more reasonable view."

Copernicus first proposed the theory that the earth encircled the sun in 1530 A.D. His proposal met with a mixture of support and violent opposition. The support resulted from the fact that he had already established his reputation as a mathematician of considerable ability. The opposition resulted from the fact that his theory was in direct conflict with the traditional view of the Roman Catholic Church, which on the authority of Aristotle put man in his "rightful" place at the center of the cosmos. The opposition ran deep. Fifty-seven years after Copernicus' death Giordano Bruno was burned at the stake for defending the heliocentric hypothesis. Martin Luther, a contemporary, chastised Copernicus, calling him a "fool" for holding views contrary to the Bible. Copernicus' response courageously admonished "those who are completely ignorant of mathematics and yet dare to judge such questions and who will blame and reject my work, relying on some badly interpreted passage of Holy Scripture."[5]

Not until new discoveries in mechanics, more accurate mathematical calculations, and the more precise astronomical observations of such thinkers as Tycho Brahe, Galileo, and Johannes Kepler in the early seventeenth century did the heliocentric hypothesis gradually begin to displace the older geocentric hypothesis that went back to Ptolemy and seemed on the face of it to accord with common sense and reason. Galileo, for example, was able to show that bodies continue to fall in straight lines even if the earth itself is in motion, and he also discovered four moons circling Jupiter in a way that seemed to provide a model of the solar system as a whole. In addition, the Copernican view was simpler, requiring only thirty-four circles to account for the motion of the earth, the moon and the planets as opposed to the seventy-nine circles required by the Ptolemaic hypothesis. The point was placed beyond reasonable doubt by Newton, whose laws of motion made it possible to explain the attraction of bodies toward the center of the earth, and the attraction of large bodies to one another across great distances. This explained why we don't fly off into space as the earth circles the sun and why the earth itself doesn't fly off into infinite space in a straight line—matters of great concern to the opponents of the heliocentric view!

In the end, the Copernican view was supported by new observations, increased accuracy, greater predictive power, simplicity, and inclusiveness in its ability to accommodate other claims—all of which, taken together, form an intelligible whole. The logical considerations of coherence and consistency, which had been acknowledged as far back as Aristotle, lent force to the new view of planetary motion.

Perhaps just as important as these considerations that led to the final acceptance of the Copernican hypothesis of planetary motion was the fact that the observations and calculations could be repeated by *anybody* at *any time*. This is the criterion of "testability," which is central to the process of verification and the establishment of claims as objective and not merely as personal beliefs.

The mass of evidence since Copernicus, and especially since Newton, has elevated the Copernican system—modified by Kepler's notion that the planets travel in elliptical orbits—to the level of truth and Kepler's original theories to laws. Such cannot be said for historical claims, as contained in the second case (C2). But the process of verification for such judgments, while certainly not as rigorous and exact, is not altogether different—as a moment's reflection will attest.

Historical Claims

Take the historical claim that "Greece and Sumeria were closely linked during the late Bronze Age." As Karl Popper has argued, historians proceed to verify this sort of claim not by tracing its sources or its origins "but [they] test it much more directly by a critical examination of what has been asserted—of the asserted facts themselves."[6] Consider the historian at work in the following passage by a contemporary American historian.

Raphael Sealey's book, *A History of the Greek City-States 700–338 B.C.*, shows innumerable examples of the procedure Karl Popper has described. For example, Sealey attempts to argue that Hesiod's *Theogony* shows close ties with the Sumerian *Epic of Kumarbi* and that therefore Greece and Sumeria were closely linked intellectually during the late Bronze Age. In supporting his claim, Sealey presents the following argument:

> The time of composition of the *Theogony* is not clear; a date in the eighth or seventh century can be defended. But the date when it

reached its present form may not be important, since it was composed orally in a traditional technique. It presents ideas of the kind which could reach Greece at the time when the alphabet was borrowed and orientalizing styles of pottery began. It is indeed conceivable that the story of the successive generations of gods was borrowed as early as the late bronze age, to which the Hittite text of *The Epic of Kumarbi* belongs, but this is less likely; the complexity of the story would not be easy to preserve in Greece of the dark ages, when contact with eastern lands was slight. The proper conclusion is that in the early archaic period, as in the late bronze age, Greece belonged to a single cultural and intellectual circle of the Near East.[7]

Consider, for the moment, the method Sealey uses in this passage. It appears that he is doing precisely what Popper says he should be doing: he is criticizing alternative points of view, rejecting those that seem unreasonable, and accepting only that conclusion that remains after criticism. Note the language of what Popper calls "critical rationalism." In this brief passage, the author uses the following key phrases: ". . . can be defended . . . ;" ". . . which could reach Greece . . . ;" "It is indeed conceivable . . . ;" "this is less likely . . . ;" and, "The proper conclusion is . . . ."

The historical method is thoroughly rational: historians look for inconsistency and incoherence—does the claim fit in with the body of accepted historical facts? If it does not, it is likely to be false. (It is possible that the body of known facts is in error, but more likely that the new claim is so.) Historians also look for evidence of bias on the part of the individuals who provide historical testimony. In rejecting Julius Caesar's accounts of the customs and social organization of the Germans, for example, the English historian/archaeologist Malcolm Todd points out that

> . . . it must be remembered that Caesar was not primarily a dispassionate ethnographer. He was an aspirant for the highest political offices and to the historian such men are dangerous.[8]

In addition, historians look for unreasonableness and unreliability of testimony and/or the sources of information at their disposal. Later in his book, for example, Sealey is critical of some claims made by the Greek historian Thucydides about the reasons for the beginnings of the Peloponnesian war. He notes that "One should be skeptical of unrealized intentions [attributed to the Spartans by the historian], especially when they are said to have been secret; such allegations could not be checked and could be invented later . . . ."[9] Indeed!

Clearly the critical methods of the astronomer and the historian differ, but it would be a mistake to focus only on the absence of mathematical proof in history and the social sciences generally and to therefore overstate those differences. The methods of the scientist and the social scientist are thoroughly rational; both seek objectivity and eschew bias, unreasonableness, and falsehood. And in both cases claims, and their grounds, are subjected to independent judgment, or "testability."

Possible Analogy with Ethics

In the sciences and social sciences, the methods of verification involve reliable methods of observation and calculation combined with a critical awareness of the context in which a claim is made and in terms of which the claim can be seen to be plausible or implausible, coherent or incoherent, consistent or inconsistent. These are methods of rational investigation that require reasonableness and reliability as determinable by *anyone* capable of undertaking the investigation. They are not subjective nor are they culturally relative.

Analogous methods are used in ethical justification, and ethical claims must be weighed and examined with the same critical scrutiny, the same insistence upon reasonableness and reliability. And the process must be repeatable by anyone at any time. Ethical claims are "objective" to the extent that the rational support they rest upon is impersonal and interpersonal and at least approximates the same standards of reasonableness and reliability we would require of any claims anywhere—whether we are determining historical accuracy or the shape of the orbits of planets.

Even though there are some problems involved in drawing parallels between science and ethics, the stubborn fact remains that some ethical claims are stronger than others; some are absurd while others approach self-evidence. More importantly, though, ethical claims can be supported by reasonable arguments and evidence that command the respect and assent of people of intelligence and good will anywhere and at any time.

Ethical Claims Examined

Let us take the case of the ethical judgment in our third example involving the radar detectors and see how we might provide a reasonable foundation for this claim. In what way can we consider the judgment "Radar detectors should be outlawed" to be a nonrelative, or objective, claim and not a merely personal belief or a claim relative to our culture?

To begin with, as we noted in the first section of this chapter, if we ask the question "why" in the face of this judgment three things can happen. In the first case the speaker simply says "I don't know. It just seems to me to be the right thing to do." In this case we are faced with a subjective claim, a claim that simply reflects the feelings of the speaker, because it lacks rational support. In the second case, the speaker may proceed to note the customs or rules that prevail in his or her culture and that lend support to the claim that such things are not approved of in that culture. In the third case, however, the speaker may list arguments and evidence to support the judgment that cut across cultural boundaries in their appeal to all rational persons. In this case we have a nonrelative claim, if, and only if, the evidence and support for the claim is not culture-bound in some way. That is, the claim purports to be true not only for our culture, but for any culture whatever. It is our job to see whether or not the support is adequate, that is, whether or not the claim can withstand critical scrutiny. We shall employ the Socratic *maieutic* and (most importantly) focus our attention on the support for the claim rather than the claim itself.

With this in mind, let us put together the strongest possible argument in favor of the proposal that "radar detectors should be outlawed," and then proceed to scrutinize that argument critically to see whether or not it appears to be based upon a firm, nonrelative foundation. We have not as yet developed the procedures to do this thoroughly, but we can use common sense and imagination. The key is whether or not the support for the claim should appeal to anybody regardless of his or her personal or cultural bias.

In the present case, then, we might encounter the following argument as support for the claim: Radar detectors should be outlawed, because their users tend to drive at higher speeds than they would otherwise and therefore run a greater risk of serious injury and even death. The greater speeds also endanger others on the highway. In addition, lower speeds have been shown to save fuel (a finite, nonrenewable energy resource) and to reduce air pollution.

Let us list these items separately:

(1) The use of radar detectors contributes to greater risk of serious injury and death [than their nonuse would].
(2) Drivers using radar detectors tend to drive faster than they would otherwise.
(3) Lower speeds conserve fuel, which is a finite, nonrenewable energy resource.
(4) Lower speeds reduce air pollution.

If we pursued the matter further, we might find that the first statement given above (involving the increased risk of serious injury and death) can be substantiated by reliable highway department statistics that correlate with the common-sense view that slower speeds are safer. The second statement supports the first and appears to be a reason for the first statement. It claims that drivers using radar detectors do, in fact, travel at higher speeds than they would without the detectors. This is a factual consideration and appears to support the first statement. In fact, the claim is supported by candid admissions on the part of the drivers themselves.

The third statement can be shown to be strong on empirical grounds, because higher speeds do tend (generally) to burn more fuel and produce more air pollution. If we attach an ethical principle (to be defended in the next chapter) to the effect that we should adopt ethical rules that increase human happiness, the conclusion that radar detectors should be outlawed appears to be quite strong. This is because the number of people made unhappy by the outlawing of detectors is small in comparison with the number of people who would be made happy by increased safety and cleaner air.

We need to add a fifth statement (as a premise) to the above list, then:

   (5) [P] One should adopt rules that increase the sum of human happiness.

For the purpose of this particular argument, we will need to add another premise. This premise is an assumption.

   (6) [A] In this instance laws should be made to enforce ethical rules.

We must note in passing that, generally speaking, the assumption that laws should be made to enforce *every* ethical rule is implausible. Because of the social consequences of the use of radar detectors, however, the assumption seems warranted in this case.

We seem to be confronted by a strong argument—one that should appeal to every reasonable person, including users of radar detectors. That is, the facts adduced to support the claim do not appear to be merely "relative." Furthermore, they seem to be able to withstand critical scrutiny, since for the most part they are collected by disinterested groups and are generally available. Whether or not this is true in the case of the ethical principle we shall see in the next chapter. But it certainly appears to be so in the case of the evidence provided: it is difficult to see how this evidence could be dismissed as "cultural bias."

In order to strengthen the argument further, we might show awareness of other points of view (some of which are strongly held) and critically consider counterarguments—knowing full well that if we weaken a counterargument we strengthen our own. We might, for example, argue against the view, sometimes held, that laws against radar detectors limit the freedom of citizens who might wish to buy and use them.

Unfortunately, this is a weak argument because it rests on the emotional appeal of the word "freedom" (we shall see why in Chapter Three). It ignores the fact that in a free society all citizens are not free to do whatever they like if what they like to do harms other members of their community. Laws also limit the freedom of citizens to set off hand grenades in crowded squares, yet we do not

DOONESBURY © 1992 by G. B. Trudeau. Reprinted with permission of Universal Press Syndicate. All rights reserved.

claim that these laws limit the freedom of would-be terrorists! To a lesser degree, this would appear to be the case with radar detectors. Laws are frequently required that limit freedom in order to benefit the majority of those affected by those laws.

It is true, of course, that outlawing radar detectors does limit one's freedom. But if the argument given here is strong—as it appears to be—there would seem to be good grounds for limiting freedom, since the freedom to use the detectors has serious social consequences that will decrease the sum of human happiness.

The claim that radar detectors should be outlawed would seem to be well argued and therefore acceptable to anybody capable of following the argument. Unless some claims have been ignored that should be considered, it would seem that we have an example of a nonrelative ethical claim. We leave it to the student to reflect on the large sums of money that have been amassed by the manufacturers of radar detectors!

Nonrelative Ethical Claims

We contend, therefore, that arguments incorporating nonrelative claims—that is, claims that can withstand criticism and scrutiny and appear to involve few, if any, personal or culturally relative factors—are binding on all rational persons regardless of cultural upbringing and personal preference. And this includes ethical arguments. A strong ethical argument, in a word, is one that should be accepted by anybody who considers it carefully, whether or not he or she *wants* to accept it.

In saying this, we must note that there is much remaining to be done to establish this thesis. We must examine thoroughly the process of justification whereby ethical conclusions pass the test of critical scrutiny. We need to arm ourselves with some basic techniques of critical reasoning that will enable us to examine ethical arguments—our own as well as those put forth by others. It might also be helpful if we consider carefully what is distinctive about *ethical* reasoning. But our first order of business is to continue our defense of nonrelativism with a look at how it is possible to reduce or eliminate personal and cultural prejudice from ethical judgments in order to make ethical claims stronger.

3. HOW OBJECTIVE CAN WE BE?

Our present objective is to defend the possibility of justifiable, cross-cultural judgments in ethics against the view of the relativist that these judgments are always and invariably personal or cultural. The defense will continue by addressing some of the views put forward by the cultural relativist that appear at first glance to be quite plausible.

For one thing, must we not admit, as the relativist contends, that our ethical claims are unavoidably saturated with personal and cultural bias? Yes and no. Ethical claims do involve personal and cultural bias in many, if not all, cases. However, as we said earlier, we are capable of reducing or eliminating personal and cultural bias in our truth claims—in ethics just as we do in science and the social sciences. As a result, these claims can reach a level of objectivity that the relativist refuses to allow.

Eliminating the subjective or cultural elements in our beliefs and claims altogether is difficult, since almost everything we say reflects our attitudes and opinions as well as the attitudes and opinions of the culture of which we are a part. This is true in the case of the most objective claims just as it is in the case of the least. To illustrate, we shall examine the way prejudice is eliminated in science—where we least expect to find it—and then proceed to draw parallels to ethics where possible. Some of the territory we traverse will be somewhat familiar, but many of the interesting points along the way may be new.

Personal Knowledge in Science

In the middle of the nineteenth century, Western science began to evidence a preoccupation with greater "objectivity." This concern surfaced in the writings of such thinkers as Ernst Mach who advanced a paradigm of science as totally free of values and personal preferences. In this view, the scientist, surrounded by increasingly sophisticated technical apparatus and supported by precise mathematical calculations, confronts an essentially dead reality and calmly, and with no personal interest in the outcome, proceeds to strip away reality's secrets until all is known.

Despite the strong appeal of relativism in other intellectual spheres, this view of science and the scientist still has its followers. It has become a bit suspect, however, as a result of the attacks upon it by such people as chemist/philosopher Michael Polanyi. In his writings, Polanyi insists that even the most exact sciences rest upon "personal knowledge," which includes such elements as passion and "the art of knowing." The latter is an "art" precisely because it can only be learned by following the example of one who hasn't the faintest idea how he or she performs the operations that are performed—often with consummate skill! In Polanyi's view, the ideal of totally objective science is a fiction.

After more than one hundred years of associating objectivity with the scientific method, however, it is difficult for many of us to accept that science, too, involves preconceptions and even prejudice. Strange as it may seem, it is not only in ethics that we must work through this maze of personal and cultural bias. Polanyi put the point well when he said:

> It is the normal practice of scientists to ignore evidence which appears incompatible with the accepted system of scientific knowledge in the hope that it will eventually prove false or irrelevant . . . there is, unfortunately, no rule by which to avoid the risk of occasionally disregarding thereby true evidence which conflicts (or seems to conflict) with the current teachings of science.[10]

Polanyi goes on to point out a common human failing that can be observed within and without scientific circles:

> Just as [in art] the eye sees details that are not there if they fit in with the sense of the picture, or overlooks them if they make no sense, so also very little inherent certainty will suffice to secure the highest scientific value to an alleged fact, if only it fits in with a great scientific generalization, while the most stubborn facts will be set aside if there is no place for them in the established framework of science.[11]

We should hasten to point out that while Polanyi rejects the pristine ideal of a totally objective science, he does insist that there is truth and objectivity in science. In connection with the Copernican theory, for example, he notes that "when we claim greater objectivity for [that theory], we do imply that its excellence is not a matter of personal taste on our part, but an inherent quality deserving universal acceptance by rational creatures."[12] He goes on to point out, in a somewhat lyrical passage, features of objective truth in science that have a direct bearing on our defense of nonrelativism in ethics. Polanyi notes that

> . . . the discovery of objective truth in science consists in the apprehension of a rationality which commands our respect and arouses our contemplative admiration; . . . such discovery, while using the experience of our senses as clues, transcends this experience by embracing the vision of a reality beyond the impressions of our senses, a vision which speaks for itself in guiding us to an ever deeper understanding of reality.[13]

Is Polanyi trying to have his cake and eat it, too? Not so. Let's be clear about what he is saying, and what he is not saying. Objectivity in science is determined by what is reasonable, what is "deserving [of] universal acceptance by rational creatures." It is not a matter of "personal taste," but it is not something fixed and immutable, standing "out there," ready-made and waiting patiently for the inquiring scientist to simply receive it and record its messages, either. What is "rational" is that "which commands our respect and arouses our contemplative admiration." We do not choose what is reasonable and what is not; it chooses us, in the sense that we find ourselves unable to reject what reason tells us is true about the world. In order to arrive at what is true we must sift through, and beyond, those attitudes and dispositions that *are* merely personal (or cultural), and find evidence and arguments that we cannot fault no matter how hard we try.

What happens in the process of scientific investigation is that prejudice, half-truths, and false preconceptions gradually give way to the superior weight of increasing evidence and greater reasonableness. It becomes increasingly difficult to defend the familiar and comfortable against the power of new evidence and more compelling arguments. We may not reach total objectivity or demonstrable certainty, but we reach a level considerably higher than that of whimsey and personal preference! The process of "coming to know" brings us closer to the truth, though we never reach a plateau that is beyond critical scrutiny. Truth in the sciences (as elsewhere) is corrigible—which means that it is subject to change and modification.

Eliminating Prejudice in Science

Let us look at the way science attempts to dislodge prejudice and establish new theories in order to (1) see how this happens, and (2) see whether or not there are lessons there to help us in ethical reasoning.

In 1923 Louis de Broglie proposed to several members of the scientific "establishment," including Paul Langevin and Charles Mauguin, the thesis that particles in motion have wave properties. The theory appealed to de Broglie, he tells us, because of its intellectual elegance and beauty, though the view was at odds with theories generally accepted at the time. The group of professors to whom the theory was suggested didn't know quite what to make of it and asked Albert Einstein for advice. Einstein immediately recognized the possibilities of the new theory and recommended that de Broglie's thesis be accepted. Mauguin later recalled that

> when the thesis was presented I did not believe in the physical reality of the waves associated with the particles of matter. I saw in them, rather, pure creations of the mind. . . . Only after the experiments of Davisson and German [in 1927], of G. P. Thompson [in 1928], and only when I held in my hand the beautiful photographs [of electron diffraction patterns from the layers of zinc oxide], which Ponte had succeeded in making in the Ecole Normale, did I understand how inconsistent, ridiculous, and nonsensical my attitude was.[14]

The same reluctance to accept a new theory hounded the Copernican view we discussed in the last section. After all, as we saw, the Ptolemaic theory accorded with common sense: we still talk about the sun "rising" and "setting." Furthermore, it placed human beings at the center of the universe; it was consistent with Aristotelian natural philosophy, which was officially recognized and accepted by the Roman Catholic Church; it was a view that had persisted for over seventeen hundred years; and it allowed for fairly accurate prediction of lunar eclipses and was, in its day, mathematically sophisticated. Additionally, it required that planets travel in perfect circular motion, which accorded with the general understanding of God's design. The new view, in contrast, required that the earth move through space at great speed in elliptical orbits—or "quasi-circles" as Copernicus called them until Kepler later identified them as ellipses. This did *not* accord with common sense or Church doctrine. However, as the evidence mounted it became increasingly clear that many of the preconceptions and convictions based on the Ptolemaic view were (at best) half-truths or (at worst) totally unacceptable. As we saw, new mathematical methods, new discoveries in mechanics, and increasingly accurate measurements made possible by the invention and use of the telescope led thinkers such as Copernicus to feel "the real necessity of substituting for the complicated Ptolemaic system some other hypothesis that would better agree with the observations, steadily growing more numerous and more accurate."[15] Some of the claims, such as the view that planets travel in perfect circular motion, were simply beliefs supported by little more than a strong desire that the belief be true, rather than by any rational evidence. Recall that Copernicus, too, was convinced that the heavenly planets must travel in circular (or "quasi-circular") orbits—so strong was this prejudice. It took a great deal of time to move this mass of conviction and displace it with the more accurate and reasonable heliocentric view. One thing that caused delay and confused even the most astute thinkers of the day was the failure to distinguish between astrology and astronomy. Kepler, for example, writing ninety years after Copernicus first proposed his view, evidenced in his writings an odd blend of astrology and astronomy, and a bit of ancient Pythagorean religious philosophy as well. He

> believed that the ratios between the maximum and minimum velocities of the planets along their orbits should be harmonic in a musical sense. Thus, for instance, he found for Saturn the major third (4/5) for Jupiter a minor third (5/6) and so on. Only the sun could hear the celestial music.[16]

It wasn't until Newton's *Principia* that the heliocentric view began to clear itself of its astrological trappings—and that book appeared over a hundred and fifty years after Copernicus first proposed his theory in 1530! Such was the weight of prejudice and tradition that accompanied the Ptolemaic view.

Progress in Science—and Ethics

There are two considerations that arise from these fairly typical examples that are of chief interest to us: First, new views must work against the great inertial force of fixed opinion, preconceptions and predispositions that are a blend of truths, comforting half-truths, falsehoods, deceptions, wishful thinking, and outright prejudice. Secondly, the new views do, surprisingly, succeed in replacing the older views, and the faulty and inadequate support that had sustained them is recognized as faulty and inadequate. In this sense, there is what we call "scientific progress."

Similarly, it makes perfectly good sense to speak about ethical progress. Just as it is no longer possible to (reasonably) insist that planets travel in circular motion, so also it is no longer possible to reasonably claim that blacks are inferior to whites, or that women are less intelligent or less able than men. The notion of "universal suffrage" no longer includes only propertied white males—as it did in the last century—but includes all persons. We no longer have autos-da-fé where heretics are publicly burned; nor do we have witch-hunts or inquisitions. We have advanced to the point in ethics that certain claims have revealed themselves as nothing more than blatant prejudice. Other biases are less obvious, but it is possible to recognize them nonetheless. Ridding ourselves of them once they have been discovered may be rather difficult, but it can be done. Recognition is the first step.

If we find ourselves supporting ethical claims with platitudes and half-truths that "we have always heard" or make us feel "comfortable," but for which we can find no rational support, or if we reject something because we find it "disgusting" or because "that sort of thing just isn't done"—but we can't say *why*—we are probably dealing with prejudice—or ignorance, at best. This does not mean that if we cannot explain why we hold onto the convictions we happen to embrace, those convictions must be falsehoods or prejudices. It means that if we cannot say why we hold these convictions we need to scrutinize them carefully for signs of prejudice and try to determine whether or not they are capable of being supported by evidence and argument. If we cannot find any argument or evidence to support them, the likelihood that they are prejudices increases.

Prejudice is embodied in a set of convictions we cling to because we are disinclined to examine them—for one reason or another. The term is variously defined, but the psychologist Gordon Allport quotes with approval the definition of prejudice as "a judgment formed before due examination and consideration of the facts—a premature or hasty judgment."[17] While strong feelings are often attached to prejudices, they always involve a "prejudgment" that is frequently based on familiarity or long-held beliefs for which we have insufficient evidence. However, something is not true simply because we have always believed it to be true, and if our innermost convictions and beliefs are not worthy of acceptance, then they should be replaced with others that are.

Relativism is unacceptable from a philosophical point of view, because it is based on oversimplification. Admittedly prejudice enters into our ethical judgments. But it does not follow that *therefore* those judgments are nothing more than a bundle of prejudices. As we have seen, we can recognize and at least partially eliminate prejudice; and we can insist upon support for our claims that is binding upon all reasonable people of good will—that is, people who are willing to keep an open mind and admit that they might be wrong. Thus, while there is an element of truth in the relativist's position, we must not mistake it for the whole truth.

Cross-cultural Judgments in Ethics

Before leaving this section, we must attend to one other element of truth in the relativist's position. We have admitted that ethical judgments are strongly influenced—though not determined—by our personal or cultural perspective. We now must also admit that cross-cultural judgments in ethics are difficult to justify. That is, ethical judgments made within one culture about activities taking place in another culture are, admittedly, problematic. As anthropologists have argued for more than a century, no one outside a particular culture can ever totally share the cultural perspective of those raised within that culture. Every culture possesses a language that is rich with tradition and layered with emotional meaning, or "connotation," that can only be grasped by those who have been raised within that culture and who have used that language from birth. In addition, there are practices, both regular and occasional, that cannot be explained to foreigners. At best, persons outside that culture can only hope to witness and enjoy these practices; they cannot ever expect to fully appreciate, much less understand, them.

Given that this is so, we must acknowledge that much of what is happening within a culture other than our own (or a subculture within our own culture) is beyond our ken. This does not mean, however, that *everything* that happens within another culture must remain opaque to outsiders and that judgments can *never* cross cultural boundaries. Once again, we must be wary of mistaking a half-truth for the whole truth.

Far too much has been made of cultural differences since anthropologists began to catalogue them in the late eighteenth century. To be sure, there are a great many such differences. Furthermore, following the lead of most anthropologists, we do want to avoid "ethnocentrism," or the view that other cultures, being different from ours, are somehow "inferior" to ours: there is no reason to allow that any culture *per se* is "superior" or "inferior" to any other culture. It may be possible to argue, however, that certain cultural *practices* are superior or inferior to others. In saying this we hasten to add that criticism cuts both ways: it is not always applicable to other cultures; some of the things we do in our culture may well elicit praise or condemnation from another cultural perspective— and that perspective may very well be clearer and more accurate than our own!

The nonrelativist does not presume that his or her cultural perspective is superior to all others; nor does he or she insist that any one cultural perspective is somehow *the* correct perspective. What nonrelativism maintains is that if persons within two different cultures utter conflicting ethical judgments, they may both be wrong but *they cannot both be correct.* The view also maintains that it is possible, and philosophically interesting, to attempt to resolve intercultural differences reasonably.

It is, of course, quite difficult to say in a particular case which of two conflicting views is the "correct" view. But we can reach reasonable conclusions in this regard. We must work through our own biases into another cultural perspective—as far as possible. And we know it can be done, because it is done almost daily.

Cultural perspectives are shared when literature written by members of one culture delights or terrifies members of another culture; it happens whenever communication takes place between men and women, blacks and whites, native people and nonnative people; it also happens whenever people raised in one culture perform music composed in another culture, and do so with sensitivity and insight. It is commonplace that "something is lost in translation"; but we must hasten to add that something is also discovered!

Cross-cultural Claims in Ethics: An Example

Though much of what people in another culture say remains "untranslatable," not all of it is. We can gain an adequate understanding and appreciation of what goes on in another culture, and at times we reason correctly that something is wrong. Let us take an example to make our case.

We know that Spartans in the fourth and fifth centuries B.C. threw weak or deformed infants from a cliff. We have a pretty good idea why the Spartans did this: they did it to purge the race of persons unfit to serve the *polis*—an idea Plato found appealing. Plutarch put it rather tersely in describing the motives of the elders of the tribe:

> . . . as thinking it neither for the good of the child itself, nor for the public interest, that it should be brought up, if it did not, from the very outset, appear made to be healthy and vigorous.[18]

Even though we cannot fully understand why the Spartans felt it necessary to do this, we can understand it well enough to say that as a practice it is rationally indefensible. There are at least two compelling reasons why the Spartans should not have engaged in this practice:

(1) Physical ability is not the only (or even the most important) measure of a person's ability to contribute to society. The Spartans, being a warlike people who found it necessary to practice the art of

war daily, placed great emphasis on physical strength and prowess. As a result, they overlooked the ways their society might have benefitted from the nonmilitary contributions of "disabled" people. This is a factual consideration that involves few, if any, "value" judgments. As such, it should appeal to persons brought up in any culture—even Spartans.

(2) Infanticide is a blatant violation of the right all persons have to life; therefore, (as we shall see) what the Spartans did was ethically wrong. And this is so whether or not the Spartans themselves recognized the rights of physically handicapped persons. We need not develop an argument to defend this claim; we need only consider that the Spartan's defense of infanticide was based on a prejudice that did not allow them to see the potential value to the Spartan *polis* of persons who are merely physically disabled. Thus, without stating any reasons to support the view that the Spartans were wrong, using the method of critical rationalism, we can show that the reasons they gave in support of the practice do not withstand scrutiny.

Most of what happens in another culture is alien to us and subject to neither praise nor blame for that reason. But occasionally it is wrong and for that reason worthy of condemnation.

The word "condemn" bothers us, however, and rightly so. The word smacks of authoritarianism and intolerance, of invasions by armies or, at the very least, by missionaries. But tolerance may not always be ethically desirable—as when onlookers tolerate the frantic cries of a stabbing victim. Furthermore, it may be nothing more than another word for "indifference," which is hardly laudable from an ethical point of view.

In conclusion, then, we can admit much of what the cultural relativist says about the nature of prejudice and the difficulties of avoiding cultural bias, without drawing the same conclusions. We reject, for example, the conclusion that what people in other cultures do is invariably right, because it cannot be accurately judged from the perspective of our culture. In addition, we can admit that we must sometimes operate in ethics through a thick mist of prejudice without accepting the conclusion that the mist cannot occasionally be reduced or penetrated by the light of reason.

There are a number of ways to cross cultural boundaries intellectually and reduce or remove our personal and cultural prejudices.

One way is to increase our awareness of and sensitivity to prejudice in its many guises; another way is to improve our critical skills so that we can recognize and appreciate strong ethical arguments that cut through the mist of bias and prejudice and transcend cultural boundaries; and finally, we can see more clearly how ethical conflict is generated and how it might be resolved by adopting an "ethical perspective," which provides us with a broader and more dispassionate point of view. Establishing this perspective will be our goal in the next chapter. Later chapters will deal with methods necessary for the analysis and evaluation of ethical arguments.

CHAPTER TWO

THE FRAMEWORK

1: RIGHTS, FAIRNESS, AND HAPPINESS: THREE TRADITIONAL PRINCIPLES IN ETHICAL DECISION-MAKING

Our word "ethics" is from the Greek *ēthikós* which is a variant of *ēthôs* meaning "custom" or, more accurately, "that which is done." Even in ancient Athens there was considerable disagreement about whether the "is" referred to what is *actually* done—as in "Einert picks his teeth after every meal"—or what is *ideally* done—as in "Einert, you shouldn't pick your teeth in public; it just isn't polite!"

If Plato is to be believed, the sophists in Athens insisted on the former interpretation and became staunch defenders of what we have labelled "relativism." They viewed ethics as a *descriptive* study that notes and catalogues the things people do, as a matter of fact. Socrates, and later Plato, and then Aristotle disagreed, insisting that ethics is *normative,* a careful and systematic investigation of the things people *should* do, regardless of cultural bias or what is considered "normal" behavior.

In the ten books of *The Nicomachean Ethics,* for example, Aristotle painstakingly analyzed the concept of *areté*, which is usually translated "virtue," but which means considerably more than we do when we use that word. *Areté* has to do with human excellence, and includes both strong character (moral virtue, according to Aristotle) and intelligence (intellectual virtue). Of central importance in Aristotle's analysis was membership in a human community, which for Aristotle, as for most Greeks, meant membership in the *polis*, or city-state. His pivotal point, and one of considerable interest to us at the moment, was that *only* through membership in a larger human community can persons achieve self-actualization, become fully human. Membership in a community produces language, thought, and culture, including manners, which are those habits that enable the community to maintain itself and the person to become happy.

Human Happiness As An Ideal

Aristotle's notion of happiness is intriguing. When he talks about happiness, Aristotle does not mean what we usually mean by the word; he is not talking about psychological happiness—about those things that give us pleasure. He is not saying what Snoopy says when he tells us that "happiness is a cold nose," or what your friend Pete says when he tells you that "happiness is in the bottle drunk." Happiness, for Aristotle, is a normative concept: it refers to those things that *ought* to make humans happy. Furthermore, happiness in this sense is not a momentary thing, like the bottle drunk or the cold nose. It is a human condition that encompasses an entire lifetime. One cannot be happy here and now; one is happy in one's total lifetime.

Aristotle ties together his notion of virtue, or human excellence, with happiness. The virtuous person is happy and *vice versa*. We become happy, in our lifetime, by making correct choices about what will in fact make us more human. For the most part, those choices can be included under the heading of moral virtue, which for the Greeks included wisdom, courage, temperance, and justice. As children our parents (and the city) help us to develop the habits of virtue—what we would call "character"—and as we grow older, we need to develop "practical wisdom," or prudence, to help us choose the correct means to those ends that will make us more human.

Is Happiness a "Dated" Notion?

All of this might sound a bit old-fashioned to the modern ear. But it is not when we translate it into today's vernacular. Aristotle is saying that good men and women are what men and women *ought* to be. They do the things that you and I wish we had done: we admire them. Clearly Aristotle has a paradigm in mind. There is an ideal of human nature toward which we ought to direct our activity, and this ideal is the same for all of us. This notion strikes us as peculiar because we have been raised to revere individuality as our ideal. But Aristotle does not rule out differences or insist that everyone be like everyone else: he merely says that everyone should be measured against the same paradigm, because human nature is one and unchanging—the same now as it was in Aristotle's day. Some people, he would say, are better than other people; they more nearly approximate that paradigm of human nature. Most of us would agree with this (in our unguarded moments, at least) and tend to measure ourselves and others against some sort of vague notion about "how people ought to act." Aristotle would simply have us develop this notion more carefully and more clearly. In doing this himself, he arrived at his notion of "virtue," which is the human good toward which all human activity ought to be directed and in terms of which all human behavior ought to be judged. As individuals we realize that ideal, or fail to realize it, in accordance with our individual capabilities and in accordance with luck, or good fortune, both of which are different for every person. If a person directs his or her life toward the highest human good, or virtue, then at the end of that person's life we can say with some confidence that he or she was "happy." Of central importance in achieving it, as we have noted, is membership in the human community.

The Human Community

Community membership involves subordination of the individual to the community of which he or she is a part—in much the same way a member of an athletic team subordinates himself or herself to the goals of the team. Subordination involves self-sacrifice but not self-denial, because membership in the community involves many more benefits than costs for the individual. Recall that for Aristotle community membership is necessary for persons to achieve their *human* potential. Exclusion from the human community, from the city-state, was anathema to the Greeks and may have been one of the reasons why Socrates chose death rather than exile from Athens.

In the community, then, the individual learns that what benefits all benefits each, and that apart from others each of us is less than human. This is the central idea behind Aristotle's ethics, generally. Membership in the human community requires a set of expectations, or norms, of interpersonal behavior. In the years since Aristotle, these norms have evolved into certain principles that have been articulated (in one form or another) by various philosophers in an attempt to produce a coherent and integrated view of what membership in the human community involves.

The view presented in this book closely follows Socrates, Plato, and Aristotle in regarding ethics as normative rather than descriptive—concerned with how we ought to behave rather than how we do behave as a matter of fact. In the ideal human community persons would respect each other's rights as persons and treat each other with fairness. Additionally, if they formulated rules to govern interpersonal activity, those rules would increase the sum of human happiness (in Aristotle's sense of that term). These are the principles we shall develop and defend in this chapter.

Three Central Ethical Principles

Our three principles encapsulate the most basic conditions that make ethical reasoning and, indeed, ethics itself possible. They focus attention on human rights, fairness, and consequences, and can be stated as follows:

(1) Treat the person in oneself and others with respect.
(2) Treat all persons fairly.
(3) Consistent with 1 and 2, adopt a rule for action that will increase the sum of human happiness.

Principle #1: Respect For Persons

The first principle owes its origin to the German philosopher Immanuel Kant, who has already been mentioned. For some, Kant's ethical view is sufficient without the addition of other principles.

But for most critics, problems result from Kant's view that necessitate the other two principles.

Kant calls moral persons "ends in themselves." The phrase stresses the importance of *respect* for persons, the cornerstone of Kant's ethical philosophy. Kant insists that we should respect moral persons and not "treat them merely as a means" to another end. That is, we ought not to use other persons for our purposes— whatever those purposes happen to be. Kant's concern for persons is primarily *negative*, leading to a series of proscriptions and leaving some room for doubt about what positive measures we should take in dealing with one another. He stresses the obligation *not* to treat persons as means; *not* to use other persons (or oneself); *not* to coerce persons, and the like. To be sure, he argues that we should promote the happiness of other persons and work to realize our own capabilities as much as possible. But while these admonitions add positive dimensions to the concept of respect for oneself and others, it is not clear how they follow from Kant's prior declaration that we treat ourselves and others as ends. This is another reason why we have augmented Kant's concept of respect for persons with two further principles.

The importance of Kant's notion of respect for persons cannot be stressed too much; indeed, we propose that it is a *necessary* condition for any ethical action. That means that if we do not respect persons, or if we act in such a way as to violate the principle of respect for persons, then we cannot claim that our action has ethical worth.

THE DIFFERENCE BETWEEN NECESSARY AND SUFFICIENT CONDITIONS

In order to understand the principle that respect for persons is a necessary condition for ethical behavior, we need to explain the difference between "necessary" and "sufficient" conditions—a distinction we borrow from Aristotle. Necessary conditions are those conditions without which something cannot be as it is: it is a necessary condition of being a bachelor that one be unmarried. But that is not sufficient. One must be both unmarried and a male, and those conditions, taken together, are sufficient to make one a bachelor.

What we are saying, then, is that respect for oneself and others is a necessary first step for an action to have ethical worth, but such respect is not by itself sufficient. As we shall see, our third principle (which presupposes the other two) is sufficient to guarantee that an action have ethical worth; each of the first two principles, taken alone or together, is necessary but not sufficient. It is not enough to respect persons; we must also treat persons fairly and adopt a rule that increases the sum of human happiness (in Aristotle's sense of that term). We shall examine the latter two principles in some detail presently. But for the moment we must discuss a problem or two in connection with our first principle.

Persons Have Rights

If we all have an obligation to respect the person in ourselves and in others, then all persons have the *right* to be respected as persons. This is so because rights, as a rule, imply correlative responsibilities, or obligations. If Barbara has a right to be treated with respect, so do all other persons, and Barbara, like everybody else, ought to respect those rights if she expects hers to be respected. Barbara's right is a natural, or human, right and it is attributable to persons simply by virtue of the fact that they are persons: they don't do anything to earn it. As Kant would have it, persons are different from nonpersons (things) in that they not only follow desire and instinct, but they have the capacity (whether or not they exercise it) to formulate, and are free to obey or disobey, moral laws. This capacity is central to what it means to be a person, and ignoring it constitutes a serious breach of the duty we all have to respect one another—such mutual respect being the bedrock of ethical behavior for Kant.

If we all have rights simply by virtue of being persons, however, is it not possible to *forfeit* those rights? That is to say, granted that we do not earn these rights and no one else can take them away from us—as Thomas Jefferson said, they are inalienable—can we not forfeit them ourselves by refusing to exercise our capacity to act morally? Can we not forfeit our right to be respected by others if, say, we commit a capital crime? Kant certainly thought this could happen.

CAN RIGHTS BE FORFEITED?

In one of his "Lectures on Ethics," Kant makes the point that

> We may have lost everything else and yet still retain our inherent worth. Only if our worth as human beings is intact can we perform our other duties; for it is the foundation stone of all other duties. A man who has destroyed and cast away his personality, has no intrinsic worth, and can no longer perform any manner of duty.[1]

The word "forfeiture" is not mentioned, of course, but clearly this is what the phrase "cast away his personality" means. The idea was not original with Kant, however, but can be found in the writings of St. Thomas Aquinas some 600 years earlier. Aquinas tells us that

> By sinning a man falls back from the level of reason, and to that extent loses the dignity of a human person free within and existing in his own right. He falls into the slavish condition of the beasts, so that he can be disposed of and treated as a utility. . . . Hence, though it is intrinsically wicked to kill a man who has kept his worth, nevertheless it may be right to put a criminal out of the way, as it is to kill an animal. Indeed, an evil man is worse than a beast and more harmful, as Aristotle says.[2]

As we can plainly see, Kant is writing within an established tradition. His words, echoing his predecessor, seem so calm and assured, straightforward and uncompromising. Unfortunately, it was not that easy. No sooner were the words we quoted above written down than Kant seemed to have second thoughts. In a later essay dealing with "Duties Toward Others," he seems to renege on his earlier position. He says that

> If a man be a rogue, I disapprove of him as a man, but however wicked he is there is still some core of good will in him, and if I distinguish between his humanity and the man himself I can contemplate even the rogue with pleasure . . . .
> No rogue is so abandoned that he does not appreciate the difference between good and bad and does not wish to be virtuous.[3]

Kant's lack of consistency here suggests that there are problems with the idea of forfeiture of rights. These problems lead us in this book to reject the notion of forfeiture, even though that rejection results in some perplexing difficulties to be touched on later.

Rights Cannot Be Forfeited

The first problem with the concept of forfeiture of rights lies in the question: "*When* does one forfeit those rights?" What constitutes a serious enough breach of respect for others to warrant the loss of one's right to be respected by others? If a man charges through the door waving a pistol and demanding all my money, can I take the poker next to the fireplace and crush his skull with impunity? Or does he have to actually take possession of my money? Or does he have to point the pistol at me and threaten to shoot? He hasn't fired the pistol at this point and, indeed, it could be unloaded or a toy and he might have been put up to this charade by some friends of mine as a practical joke. (I have some strange friends!) Or does the man forfeit his right when he has fired the pistol and killed someone? Or does he forfeit it later, when the jury finds him guilty? But what if the jury makes a mistake? He is seen leaving the scene of the crime with a smoking gun in his hand, but someone else is mistaken for him and that person is subsequently tried and convicted of the murder and summarily executed. If we discover that this happened we might say, "Gee, I'm sorry! It seems we made a mistake!" Mistakes happen and often innocent people are found guilty of crimes they didn't commit. We ask again: When, exactly, does forfeiture happen?

The second problem is whether or not forfeiture is final. This seems to be the question Kant was struggling with in the second passage quoted above. Is it right to take other people's lives when they have forfeited their right to be respected as persons because of, let us say, a criminal act about which there can be no doubt? Or is it possible that by virtue of some future act they could redeem themselves twice over? Suppose, as the Russian novelist Dostoevsky did while writing *Crime and Punishment*, that his murderer-hero Raskolnikov rushes into a burning building and saves the life of a little girl. Does that constitute redemption? Or is it not possible—

ever under any circumstances—for the criminal to *regain* lost self-respect and the respect others once owed him?

These are not outrageous, off-the-wall sorts of questions. They go to the heart of the doctrine of forfeiture, and they raise serious questions about whether or not the doctrine makes any sense. We consider them serious enough in this book to argue that a person *always* has the right to be respected and can never lose that right no matter what he or she does, appears to have done, or is charged with doing. That's why we consider the principle of respect for persons a necessary condition for ethics; it is the cornerstone of our ethical theory.

RIGHTS ARE ABSOLUTE

One of the very few philosophers to have "bitten the bullet" on the issue of non-forfeiture of rights and to take seriously the inviolability of the person is the twentieth-century American philosopher Eliseo Vivas. In his most interesting book *The Moral Life and The Ethical Life*, Vivas insists that human beings have a status unique among all the things in this world, namely their status as persons, and their moral personality cannot be lost or cast away. This fact is only acknowledged by "the ethical man," however, who, through suffering, has been made aware of the special status of persons. Vivas tells us that

> . . . there resides in the person an intrinsic worth distinct from the total worth of the values he espouses.

He explains by saying that

> . . . the ethical man respects the other person and treats him in such a way as to avoid violating his dignity, no matter how unworthy morally he may be known to be. For him, beyond moral distinctions lies the intrinsic worth of a man which neither vice nor weakness nor accident can annihilate.[4]

Admittedly, there are problems with the claim that the status of persons is somehow absolute and that no one at all, not even Saddam Hussein or Charles Manson, ever loses the dignity that must always attach itself to persons. But, then—as we have seen—there are problems with the idea of forfeiture as well. From an ethical perspective the problems with the absolute status of persons appear to be less serious than do those of forfeiture. However, this issue we shall leave for the reader to decide. In the meantime, we shall return to several other issues surrounding the concept of personhood that we previously left in the air.

Self-Respect and Using Others As a Means to an End

To begin, we shall examine what it means to *use* other persons and discuss the notion of respect for oneself, which is incorporated into our first principle.

Please recall that we are still attempting to grasp the Kantian notion of persons as ends. Even though we might disagree with Kant over whether respect for persons can be forfeited, we still unconditionally embrace his concept of persons as worthy of respect. In this regard, one of the best discussions of what Kant might have meant by his odd phrase "using others as a means to another end," has been provided by Onora O'Neill, who singles out coercion as one common way persons use other persons, thereby violating the principle of respect for persons. O'Neill does not claim that the only way persons use one another is by coercion, but she may be right that the phenomenon is more common than we might like to admit.

Briefly stated, coercion involves the denial of the status of the other as a person, of the other's autonomy, or self-determination. If, for example, Fred demands that his wife quit her job and stay home, with no regard for what his wife wants, we have a case of coercion. Coercion, then, is in direct opposition to consent. As O'Neill puts it,

> Morally significant consent will, I suggest, be consent to the deeper or more fundamental aspects of another's proposals. . . . [T]o treat others as persons we must allow them *the possibility of consent or dissent* from what is proposed . . . *making their consent or dissent possible.*

O'Neill argues that respect for persons goes further than simply avoiding coercion; it is a positive obligation as well. Kant would doubtless agree with O'Neill when she says that

> To treat human beings as persons . . . we must not only not use them, but we must take their particular capacities for autonomy and rationality into account.[5]

Coercion, then, denies not only the personhood (autonomy and rationality) of others, but also our *own* when, for example, we *allow* others to coerce us and otherwise use us for their purposes. When we know others are lying or deceiving us, or manipulating us psychologically or physically, it is wrong not to resist such manipulation. Self-respect involves the insistence upon being respected by others and it is, according to the view defended here, at least as important as our obligations to others. As Kant would have it, we cannot acknowledge our other obligations unless we first acknowledge our obligation to ourselves as persons.

It might be argued, however, that we have not really tested the principle of mutual respect for persons, and we cannot therefore consider it to be a viable ethical principle. That is true. Think about it for a moment, though: what would it *mean* to reject a principle that is a necessary condition for ethical behavior? That would amount to a rejection of ethics itself, which is absurd. But suppose we were to simply deny that respect for persons *is* a necessary condition for ethics? This is a very difficult question, so let us proceed slowly.

To say that respect for persons is not a necessary condition for ethics is to say that we could treat one another ethically without mutual respect. But what would that involve? If we can make any sense out of this notion at all, it would seem to mean we would treat one another ethically (i.e., we would avoid harming one another, we would treat another fairly and honorably, etc.) not because we *ought* to do so, but because we *want* to. If we don't happen to want to, however, presumably, we wouldn't. In a word, denial of respect for persons would make ethical behavior totally arbitrary and whimsical. It would in all likelihood reduce human interaction to a struggle for power, which is to say, it would involve a rejection of ethics once again.

Principle #2: Fairness to Others

We mentioned earlier, you may recall, that the principle of respect for persons, while being a necessary condition of ethical behavior, is not adequate by itself to assure that a given action will have ethical worth. For one thing, it is not clear in a concrete case just what "respect for persons" might involve. Obviously, we ought not to lie and coerce people; we ought not to harm them, either. But we need more than simply the principle of respect for persons, even if we grant that this includes, following Onora O'Neill, taking "their particular capacities for autonomy and rationality into account." We need a principle of *fairness* that will allow us to acknowledge more fully some of the *positive* obligations we have to one another. Let us see how the second principle adds dimensions to our present discussion, especially when ethical conflict involves more than one or two people.

Recall the dialogue that forms the prelude to this book. In that dialogue Nina suggests to Rick that students be graded according to where they sit in the classroom. Rick is, understandably, outraged and shouts that "it wouldn't be fair!" He's right, of course, and that's Nina's point. In a sense, though, the rights of the students have been acknowledged in that each of them has the opportunity to sit in the front of the class and get an "A." But what the situation conceived by Nina creates is the "right" of each student to be treated unfairly. This is unacceptable. Most of us would insist that the students are not being treated with respect, because the situation reduces itself to a battle for front row seats. Whether or not this is true, it is even clearer, as Rick insists, that the situation is not fair. Thus, we introduce the principle of fairness to supplement the principle of respect for persons in borderline cases in which it is not clear just what respect for persons entails.

We could argue that the principle of fairness is contained, somehow, in the principle of respect for persons, in that we cannot be unfair to someone and *at the same time* have respect for them. To a certain extent this is true. But we stated the second principle in a positive way (treat all persons fairly) rather than negatively (do not treat persons unfairly) in order that we might draw attention to the positive dimensions of ethics, dimensions that might be ignored if we focus exclusively on the concept of respect for persons—which, as we saw, generates a list of *proscriptions* rather than a list of *prescriptions,* things we should avoid rather than things we should do.

"Fairness" is not an especially difficult concept to accept, and this is another reason to introduce it. It seems to be most helpful when we are dealing with groups of people—it is not clear much of the time what it means to be fair to a particular person in a specific situation, unless we mean simply not to be disrespectful—and it is easy to grasp on an intuitive level, even in childhood. For example, if we make the mistake of giving a little girl a smaller piece of cake than her friends, she will cry out, "It isn't fair!" And she will be right! She is learning about discrimination, which is what happens when our second principle is ignored; and if the other children happen to be boys, she is probably learning about sexual discrimination!

Fairness requires that we treat others as we would have them treat us, that we apply the same standards to and have the same requirements of all persons. It demands that we not only respect one another but that we treat one another with consideration and sympathy. Fairness requires that in life, as in games, we all play "by the same rules"—both written and unwritten.

Adding the second principle, then, assures us that two necessary conditions are made explicit, both of which help to provide content to what might otherwise be a rather abstract and unsatisfactory admonition to maximize the sum of human happiness. This is our third principle and we need to examine it in some detail.

Principle #3: Adopt Rules That Increase the Sum of Human Happiness

This principle is an adaptation of what is called "rule utilitarianism," which is an attempt by contemporary philosophers to improve upon the "act utilitarianism" of Jeremy Bentham. As initially put forward by Bentham in the early part of the nineteenth century, utilitarianism tended to direct attention away from motives and actions themselves and toward the consequences of actions. Bentham was convinced that the rightness of an action was a function of how many people were made happy by that action. The more people an action made happy, the better it was. By "happy," Bentham meant "pleased," and he was convinced that we could weigh and measure alternative courses of action and choose the one that produced the most pleasure, that was, therefore, the right action.

Bentham's nephew, John Stuart Mill, was also an act utilitarian, but he found that this simplistic equation of happiness with pleasure yielded some rather peculiar conclusions—such as the conclusion that an hour at an orgy is better (in a moral sense) than an hour of reading Aristotle's *Metaphysics*, because it is more pleasant (present company excepted!). Mill, therefore, rejected the identification of happiness as pleasure, though he retained Bentham's concern with consequences. He accepted the idea that right actions maximize *human* happiness—those things that contribute to making us more "virtuous" in Aristotle's sense of that term as we explained it above. (Presumably, human beings would not be as happy at an orgy as they would reading Aristotle, even though they might find it more pleasant. That is, such an action would not contribute to human excellence. In any event, pleasure was no longer the measure of the rightness of an ethical action for Mill.)

The major improvement the rule utilitarians made to Mill's version of act utilitarianism was to direct attention away from specific actions and their consequences to the rules that govern actions. The need for rules—not to mention a recognition of human rights—is suggested in the Doonesbury cartoon printed here. Act utilitarianism appears in the guise of a "cost/benefit" analysis that leaves too many questions unanswered.

Adopting Ethical Rules

What is the advantage of focusing attention on the adoption of a rule for an action rather than on the action itself? How is rule utilitarianism an advance over traditional (act) utilitarianism? In either case, we are primarily concerned that the consequences of actions be taken into consideration in determining the ethics of actions. But in Mill's version of utilitarianism, focusing as it does on specific actions, certain puzzling implications strike us as soon as we consider specific cases.

Suppose, for example, Fred lends Alice $50. But instead of paying him back when the money is due, Alice gives the $50 to a charity for cancer research. In Mill's view the charitable act is

DOONESBURY

DOONESBURY © 1992 by G. B. Trudeau. Reprinted with permission of Universal Press Syndicate. All rights reserved.

ethically correct because it makes more people happy than the alternative of repaying the debt. But the rule utilitarian would insist that this is not the right thing to do, because if one were to adopt a rule that this sort of thing should be done as a matter of course, it would produce less happiness than if it weren't done and the debt were repaid. And here we are in agreement with the rule utilitarian. We would say that the act of repaying the debt is the right thing to do because—bringing all three of our principles to bear—the charitable action (1) violates the promise Alice made to Fred when she borrowed the money, and therefore violates the principle of respect for him as a person; (2) is not fair because it violates the tacit rules of lending and borrowing; and (3) cannot be viewed as right because if we adopted such a rule it would not maximize the sum of human happiness, which necessitates honesty and the keeping of promises. This last point is supported by the observation that if everyone were to refuse to repay debts and give the money to charity instead then it would no longer be possible for people to borrow money when in need. As a result, the fabric of trust that lending and borrowing rest upon would be shredded—and this has serious implications that go beyond lending and borrowing. Add to this the observation that it is unlikely that Alice's donation will bring about a breakthrough in cancer research and we can see what the conclusion must be.

The genius of Gary Trudeau's cartoon lies in the fact that President Bush is having difficulty finding a rule or principle that would justify the invasion of Panama. This underscores the inadequacy of a simple "cost/benefit," or act utilitarian, analysis. It is difficult, perhaps impossible, to adopt an ethical rule that would ignore the rights of human beings to be recognized as persons. This difficulty nicely demonstrates the need for our first principle.[6]

The Application of the Three Principles

The first principle draws attention to the status of persons, who are invariably involved in ethical conflict. The second principle supplements the first and allows us to consider numbers of persons and to resolve some of the conflicts that arise between and among the obligations that persons have to one another. Each of these principles is a necessary condition for ethical action, in that actions cannot be ethical if they violate either of these principles. But a third principle is required to draw attention to consequences of actions and to make possible the weighing of alternatives and the rational determination of which of our options is ethically correct, that is, more likely to increase the sum of human happiness.

We shall see how these principles work in concrete cases later in the book.

Food for Further Thought

You may or may not accept the principles proposed above. It is difficult to argue for principles, though the view presented here that ethics has to do with our membership in the wider human community does provide a basis for the principles advanced in this chapter. We need to consider what membership in the human community involves—how are we to get along with other human beings and at the same time become more human? The three principles we have proposed are designed to answer this question, but you should weigh this answer critically. If you were to reject one or more of these principles, would you substitute others? Or would you insist that ethical principles are out of place? Some of the things we have said about the first principle, at least, are troublesome, to put it mildly.

Can we say that "respect for persons" is a necessary condition for ethics? Does this make any sense? Is it a defensible position? If, for example, a lie is a violation of the respect we should have for one another, what about a lie told to save a person's life? What if, let us say, a good friend were hiding in your basement to escape an angry mob and you were asked a direct question by the mob's leader about your friend's whereabouts. Should you tell the truth? Surely not! Some would argue that you have an obligation to lie in such a case.

In the view presented here, however, this is not so. Our position maintains that the mob leader has a right to the truth, even though he plans to harm or possibly kill the man hiding in your basement. There is a painful conflict here, and we shall argue in the fifth chapter that in such cases of "tragic conflict" there is *no* ethically right action: we can only choose the lesser of two evils. This does not mean that, as a matter of fact, you would not lie in this case. It simply means that you could not claim on philosophical grounds that you had done the *right* thing to lie. The lie could not be justified in this case, because it is wrong—even though it is the lesser of two evils.

Not everyone would accept this, of course. It may be totally wrongheaded. The English philosopher R. M. Hare belittles the notion of "tragic situations" because he thinks that such situations arise out of a conflict between or among intuitions and that once we reason critically (by applying what he calls the method of "universalization" correctly) the conflict will be resolved. But does this really get us around the central issue? That is, when we call an action that can be universalized "right," does this alter the fact that it may simply be the lesser of two evils—which is to say that from another perspective that same action can also be viewed as "wrong"?

And what about the claim that human rights cannot be forfeited? Does that seem plausible to you? Suppose, for example, the police capture a man who has confessed to killing seventeen young boys after molesting and torturing them? Doesn't it seem ethically right to demand that the man forfeit his life? Isn't capital punishment justified in this case?

Think about the point made in the text, though. Is there *nothing* the man can do to redeem himself? Can he do nothing—ever—to make amends? To be sure, his subsequent actions will not bring the boys back to life; but, then, neither will his execution. Can we *justify* capital punishment, in this case or in any other case? Is capital punishment ever right? If so, why? The position taken here is that it is never right. What do *you* think?

2: THE ETHICAL PERSPECTIVE

In the last section we suggested three principles that comprise the ultimate basis of ethical argument. As we seek to incorporate these principles into our thinking about ethical conflict and ethical choices, we will need to adopt a slightly different perspective than we do in our ordinary thinking. We shall call this the "ethical perspective," in which (in the words of Jeremy Bentham) "everybody counts for one, and none of us for more than one."

Of central importance in ethical thinking is the displacement of the self from a place of special privilege. Ethical thinking is "prescriptive." That is to say, when choices are made in ethics, they are not based on what is right *for me*, they are based on what is right *for anybody*. To take an earlier case, it is not merely right for me to avoid using radar detectors; if our argument is sound, it is right for everybody to avoid using radar detectors. The same is true for the case of infanticide: if our argument is correct then it was wrong for the Spartans to engage in this practice *even though they would not admit it.*

The prescriptive element in ethical argument bothers many people. It smacks of intolerance in an age that prides itself on its tolerance and its willingness to allow each person to "do their own thing." But think about it for a moment. If I make the ethical judgment "Sally really shouldn't have murdered the milkman," and if the reasoning that supports this judgment is sound, then it is true for me, for you, for Sally, and for anybody else, that what Sally did was wrong. The key element here is contained in the little word "if." It allows us to avoid intolerance in ethics: we are all bound by the conclusion *if* (and only if) the reasoning is sound.

We have seen how difficult it is to avoid prejudice in ethics—and elsewhere. We shall soon see how difficult it is to justify our ethical judgments, that is, to support them with facts and sound argumentation. The process of ethical argumentation is fundamentally open-ended. We can never be certain that our judgments are free of prejudice or that the reasoning that supports them is totally sound. That is why we must remain tolerant and acknowledge human fallibility. But because we reject relativism and the attendant notion that ethical judgments are true for you but not necessarily true for me, we are committed to the view that we are all bound by the strength of the argument support for those judgments. This places considerable burden on the process of ethical argumentation and necessitates a firm understanding of what makes an ethical argument sound. Explaining this will be our objective in the chapters that follow. In this section we need to focus carefully on that perspective that is unique to ethics and which will enable us to think more clearly about ethical matters: the ethical perspective.

Features of the Ethical Perspective

The ethical perspective involves three aspects:

(1) a concern for the consequences of one's actions,
(2) neutrality, and
(3) imagination, which allows us to put ourselves in the place of others who happen to be the victims of ethical wrong-doing.

Except for the third aspect, in which such feelings as outrage, compassion and empathy are clearly involved, the ethical perspective requires that we become *distanced* from the ethical conflict in order to eliminate bias or prejudice as much as possible. In the words of R. M. Hare, we must move from the "intuitive level" to the "critical level" of moral reasoning in order to resolve ethical conflict. As Hare notes, "although the relatively simple principles that are used on the intuitive level are necessary for human moral thinking, they are not sufficient."[7] The ethical perspective helps us move to the critical level in our ethical thinking.

This is not to say that "gut feelings" and moral intuitions are out of place in ethics, or that they should be removed in the critical process along with bias, superstition, and fear. It simply means that we must deal with them critically, since even the strongest feelings are not always totally reliable. To be sure, our gut reaction to such things as cruelty and insensitivity in our fellow human beings can indicate the presence of ethical problems: reactions are an excellent starting place for ethical reflection, but we must resist the temptation to trust those feelings without subjecting them to critical scrutiny. As the contemporary psychologist James Hillman has said:

> The terrorist and the girl who kills for her cult hero (Charles Manson) also trust their feelings. Feelings can become possessed and blind as much as any other human function . . . Feelings are not a faultless compass to steer by; to believe so is to make Gods of them, and then only good Gods, forgetting that feeling can be as instrumental to destructive action and mistaken ideologies as any other psychological function.[8]

Thinking is not infallible, either, but it is a necessary corrective to misguided feelings.

We can all readily admit how much easier it is to think clearly and dispassionately about people who have lived in the distant past and with whom we have no direct connection. Time and place can afford a natural distance, but it is also possible, if we adopt the ethical perspective, to achieve a degree of distance even in the face of immediate personal conflict. Let us, then, examine in some detail how the ethical perspective functions.

Feature #1: Concern for Consequences

As a general rule, most of us are motivated, most of the time, by short-run self-interest. We want what we want when we want it, and we want it NOW! Unfortunately, from the ethical perspective, such short-run thinking has little bearing on ethical outcomes. In ethics it is essential that persons who would do the right thing consider the consequences of their actions. This means that if we are to act ethically we must attend to the long run and consider long-run, or "enlightened," self-interest rather than short-run self-interest.

No one on earth knows better than you what you want. You are, therefore, the ultimate authority on what is in your own *short-run* self-interest. Nevertheless, there are things that we all *need*, and these things are not necessarily what we want. When we distinguish between what we want and what we need, we shift attention from short-run to long-run self-interest and we must acknowledge that none of us is necessarily the ultimate authority on matters of long-run self-interest. The consideration of consequences requires thought, imagination, and, at times, the advice of others. To take a simple example, few of us want the dentist to drill a tooth, but we all recognize the fact that at times we need just that.

Short-run self-interest is narrowly focused on the here and now. Since long-run self-interest incorporates a concern for needs as well as desires, it has a broader focus. As mentioned, it is sometimes referred to as "enlightened" self-interest, and it centers around our membership in the human community which, as we saw in the last section, is of vital concern in ethics. Short-run self-interest, in contrast, has little (if anything) to do with ethics, since it focuses on the individual in isolation from others.

Mark Slackmeyer has been interviewing members of the "Homeless Community" in Lafayette Park at Thanksgiving time, a time described as "the highlight of the homeless social season . . . . . Hot turkey, cranberry sauce, the works!" The group is to be entertained by the "Dumpster Divers," and in this panel Mark is interviewing one of the members of that group. As Trudeau points out, it is not always easy to consider the "long term"! DOONESBURY © 1992 by G. B. Trudeau. Reprinted with permission of Universal Press Syndicate. All rights reserved.

Above all else, the ethical perspective has at its center the idea of what we *ought* to want, what we need as human persons or members of the human community. The moment we begin to reflect on the consequences of our actions, we begin to take others into account. The more we consider the consequences of our actions in the long run the more we realize that our own self-interest is bound up with the interest of others. Our needs are almost always *human* needs, as we saw in the last section. Let us, however, be clear about the other two aspects of the ethical perspective as mentioned above.

Feature #2: Neutrality

The ethical perspective also incorporates impartiality, or neutrality, as we consider the effects of our actions upon others, all of whom count equally. That is, we should consider the claims of all persons as equally binding and none as any more basic than any others— and this includes our own claims as well. No one counts for any more than anyone else from the ethical perspective—not you, not me, and not even your great Aunt Tilly who will surely leave you a small fortune when she dies!

In his important book *A Theory of Justice,* John Rawls was apparently intent on incorporating this notion of impartiality into his argument. He proposed the notion of "the original position of equality," which requires that each of us consider questions of fairness and justice through a "veil of ignorance." Behind this veil we lack any particular knowledge about any of the individuals who are involved in the ethical conflict we are addressing; we cannot pursue our own short-run self-interest, because we don't know what that is! Behind the veil of ignorance I do not know whether I am rich or poor, black or white, male or female, victim or victor. The notion stresses the fundamental ethical equality of all human beings in the original position. As Rawls put it, ". . . with this adjustment no one is able to formulate principles especially designed to advance his own cause. Whatever his temporal position, each is forced to choose for everybody."[9]

We must consider all persons equally in determining the rightness or wrongness of possible actions and, as the agent of ethical actions, we must not be biased in our own favor. It is this feature of the ethical perspective, more than any other, that generates a respect for all persons and makes us aware that ethical concerns are global. This awareness is sharpened by the third aspect of the ethical perspective.

Feature #3: Imagining Oneself as Victim

With the exception of thinkers such as R. M. Hare, philosophers seldom consider the importance of imagination in ethics; but, as Hare insists, it is central. Intuitively, the easiest way for one to see that an action is wrong in a particular case is to imagine that it is being done to oneself. This, one might suppose, is the point of the so-called "Golden Rule," to do unto others as we would have them do to us. For example, I would be less likely to steal if I were to imagine that I am the one stolen from, less likely to cheat and lie if I imagine myself the one cheated and lied to, and less likely to discriminate if I imagine myself the victim of discrimination. To quote R. M. Hare once again, "it is [knowledge of what it is like for the person wronged] which, I am proposing, we should treat as relevant, and as required for the full information which rationality in making moral judgments demands."[10]

Hobbes is helping Calvin imagine himself to be a victim of unethical conduct!
CALVIN AND HOBBES © 1989 by Universal Press Syndicate. Reprinted with
permission. All rights reserved.

The three aspects of the ethical perspective—concern for the consequences of our actions, impartiality, and the ability to imagine oneself the victim of ethical wrongs—combine to help us determine whether a proposed action is right or wrong. We must note, however, that the ethical perspective is nothing more than an aid to intuition. As such this device does not *demonstrate* that a proposed course of action is right or wrong, but it does enable us to place an action in its context and see the implications of that action more clearly than we would otherwise. Furthermore, when used in conjunction with the techniques of critical thinking that we shall develop in the next chapter, the ethical perspective can be extremely beneficial in helping us to resolve ethical disputes reasonably.

A Case in Point

Let us take a simple example to see how the ethical perspective works, remembering that what we say is preliminary and in need of further amplification in later chapters.

Let us suppose that I owe you $50 and, since I just got paid today and I know that you need the money to pay some of your bills, it would appear that I am obliged to repay you the money owed. As it happens, however, my wife suggests that it would be fun to go out to dinner and a movie. Since I haven't gone out with her for a while, I decide to accept her offer. Unfortunately, after I have paid my bills and spent the money for the dinner and the movie I will not have $50 left to repay you. Should I take my wife out for the evening? If we examine the question from the ethical perspective the answer seems clear: it would be wrong. There really is no argument on the side of taking my wife out for the evening: I simply *want* to do so. This is nothing more than short-run self-interest and does not count from the ethical perspective, from which the obligation to repay the debt is quite strong—as a moment's reflection will attest. (1) The long-run consequences of not repaying the money I owe you involve inconvenience and even possible harm to you, since for all I know you may owe money to others. In addition, even from a narrow, selfish viewpoint I may not be able to borrow money from you, or anyone else, if I don't repay my debts. (2) If I think about it even briefly I would have to admit that if I didn't *want* to have an evening out with my wife (using your money) the issue would never have come up. Thus, I have a decided interest in the matter. Finally, (3) I would certainly not like you to go out for the evening with money you owed *me*. All three dimensions of the ethical perspective converge to impress upon me the obligation to repay the debt. Thus, what I *ought* to do is to repay the debt. But is this what I *would* do?

Being Ethical Often Conflicts with Being Practical

The answer to this question is "perhaps so, perhaps not." In the "real" world we rarely do what we should do, unfortunately. But there is a fundamental difference between determining what we *ought* to do and determining what we probably *will* do. This point is related to the rejection of short-run self-interest as an ethical reason. Much of what we do (in fact) is, as we have noted, motivated by what we want to do; ethics, however, requires that we carefully consider those things that we ought to do—whether or not we want to do them. Let us consider the difference between ethical considerations and considerations of short-run self-interest a bit further.

The gap between what people determine to be the right thing to do and what they do in fact is worthy of mention. Often situations demand that we "keep our mouth shut," or "toe the line," and it becomes difficult to do the ethical thing even though we know with some certainty what should be done. But this is a *psychological* problem, not a philosophical one. The fact that one has difficulty doing what one has determined to be right has nothing to do with the question of how we determine what the right thing is. It has to do with the need to reconcile ourselves to the fact that at times we must do what we know is wrong.

Thus, even though we must be "realistic" and "practical" and recognize that people do not often (seldom?) do what they should do, (what they think is ethically right), we must continue to focus on the ethical reasoning process itself, rather than on the practical problems of actually doing the right thing. Saying that an action is not practical does not mean that it is not right. Philosophy can be enlightening and useful in ethical conflict by helping us to determine what the ethical option happens to be. But philosophy cannot help us to direct our actions in accordance with that option.

We acknowledge that ethical reasoning may well be ineffective because our society, and the workplace in particular, does not place a premium on ethical behavior. But that is no criticism of the *reasoning process* that simply helps us determine in a given case what the right course of action is. Most of us easily follow the course of action that is in our short-run self-interest. Ethics is frequently, if not always, in conflict with short-run self-interest. That is what makes it so hard to do the right thing.

Short-Run Self-Interest and Duties to Oneself

To say, however, that short-run self-interest does not count as an ethical reason requires argument. It is certainly not self-evident, and a number of ethical theorists would disagree with this claim. Whatever support we might find for the claim would probably incorporate some of the features of the ethical perspective described here, such as our claim that ethical reasoning requires neutrality and centers around a concern for others, for the human community, if not the community of all living creatures. A hermit would have few, if any, ethical conflicts: the formation of societies and human communities generally imposes on all who would be members of those communities certain ethical obligations, as we saw in the last section. At the moment we need to stress that the difficulty with short-run self-interest is that it ignores others and focuses on the self in isolation: "You don't really matter; I'm the only one who counts!" The person who thinks this way has not adopted the ethical perspective and is likely to do the right thing only accidentally, if at all.

Those who want to hang onto the notion of short-run self-interest as a legitimate ethical reason would insist that it makes perfectly good sense to talk about "ethical egoism," or the view that we have ethical obligations to do whatever is best for ourselves—not necessarily what we want for ourselves. The important notion here is the implied claim that we all have duties to ourselves (even the hermit), and it would appear that by ruling out short-run self-interest as a legitimate ethical reason we are ignoring those duties. We are, it might be said, members of the human community ourselves—or most of us are—and we have the same duties toward ourselves that we have toward anyone else. Thus, if we recognize our duties to others as legitimate ethical reasons, then we should acknowledge the legitimacy of short-run self-interest as well.

Our position, on the contrary, is that we can acknowledge our duties to ourselves without bringing in the notion of short-run self-interest. From the ethical perspective we acknowledge that all persons should be regarded as having the same claims. Therefore, to be sure, we have duties to ourselves. But short-run self-interest is not a "duty"; it is something we *want*. Thus, we can count the duties we have to ourselves as legitimate ethical concerns while, at the same time, we ignore short-run self-interest. Further, since we have strong natural inclinations to do what we want to do, we don't need to claim ethical status for what we want to do anyway!

Food for Further Thought

Before reading any further you should carefully consider whether or not you accept the claims we have made thus far. Are you willing, for example, to accept the claim that short-run self-interest does not count as an ethical reason? It does not count, we are saying, because ethics requires that we adopt a neutral stance. From that stance we find compelling only those reasons to undertake a course of action that would persuade anyone *else* that it is the right thing for him or her to do as well. Personal calculations and practical considerations, we are saying, are *irrelevant* to the ethical question, because they are simply matters of short-run self-interest. Do you agree with this?

Psychological Egoism

Another question worth considering is the following: even if we grant that short-run self-interest does not count as an ethical reason, is it *possible* for a person who wants to do the ethically right thing to do so? Or are all motives really motives of short-run self-interest in disguise? If people do everything for reasons of self-interest—a view called "psychological egoism"—then it is not possible for anyone to have "ethical reasons," or reasons that reflect a concern for other persons, or are at times in direct conflict with self-interest.

The view of psychological egoism is extremely difficult to refute because even if we find other motives operating in particular situations, the view insists that *real motives* are frequently unconscious, hidden even from the person himself or herself. Thus, if a woman, say, were to decide to tell the truth because she found the reasons to do so persuasive, the psychological egoists would dismiss this entire process as a sham. According to them, all of us simply do what we want to do, nothing more and nothing less. Any attempts to find other reasons for our actions—such reasons as duties to others or to ourselves—are merely various forms of self-deception and subterfuge that allow us to fool ourselves into thinking we are good people when we are simply doing what we want to do. Psychological egoists consider ethical argumentation, as a whole, a form of self-delusion.

What do you think? Can you think of any personal experiences that seem to fly in the face of psychological egoism? What about second or third person experiences? Are there no selfless motives? Suppose, for example, a starving mother in Nigeria grabs a crust of bread and, instead of wolfing it down herself, gives it to her child. Is it accurate to say that she acted out of self-interest? Or is it more accurate to say that she was primarily concerned about her child? We might agree that she gets satisfaction from the act, but her satisfaction followed her action and does not appear to have been the motive for it. Does this example constitute disproof of psychological egoism? If not, what would refute a theory that makes ethics impossible? What about a young soldier who throws himself on a hand grenade to save his fellow soldiers? Would such an example be a problem for the psychological egoist? Or *is* ethics impossible, a form of self-delusion?

MOTIVE

You must consider one final point before you leave this section: the "ethical perspective" as it is presented here totally ignores the question of motive. Do you think motive should be considered a part of any position that professes to provide a perspective on ethical issues? Immanuel Kant, for example, insisted that motive was at the heart of ethics. The classical attack on Kant's view was presented by G. E. Moore early in this century when he insisted (following a view not altogether unlike the one presented here) that good motives make actions "praiseworthy" but only consequences make them "right." For example, if a physician tries to save a patient's life by administering a drug and in doing so kills the patient, Moore would say that the physician's motive was praiseworthy, but he did not do the right thing. What do you think? If the psychological egoist is right, of course, we cannot have ethical motives: we all act out of self-interest, simply. But if the psychological egoist is wrong and there are ethical motives— obligations to do the right thing—can we talk about an "ethical perspective" without considering motives?

In the last chapter, we borrowed a principle from Kant that insists upon respecting persons, but we do not agree with him that motive is of central importance in ethics. However, the important question here is: what do *you* think?

INTERLUDE: RICK AND NINA REVISITED

RICK: I've been thinking about our talk the other day and there are a couple of things that continue to bug me.

NINA: Oh? Like what, for instance?

RICK: Well, like the fact that people who think there's some kind of absolute right and wrong tend to be dogmatic and intolerant. I'm not saying *you* are, but people who take your point of view frequently are. If there's one thing we've learned from history it's that people who think they've got the "truth" about how other people should live their lives tend to go around shoving their ideas of right and wrong down everyone else's throat!

NINA: I don't blame you. That sort of thing has always bothered me, too. But what people do when they think they've "got the truth" (as you put it) doesn't affect the question of whether they do or do not know something you and I might not know. After all we don't know everything!

RICK: Neither do they. That's what bugs me.

NINA: They might not know everything, but they could still know something you and I don't know. We've got to be careful that we don't confuse two separate issues, though.

RICK: What two issues?

NINA: First, whether it makes sense to say that people can know if there is a right and wrong when it comes to human actions, and, second, why they behave as they often do when they think they *do* know!

61

RICK: OK. Let's agree that these are two separate issues. How do we deal with them?

NINA: Well, I'd ignore the second issue. I'm not qualified to say why people tend to become intolerant when they think they know something someone else doesn't know—especially when it comes to right and wrong. But, I do think it makes perfectly good sense to say that people *can* reason about right and wrong and that they can reach reasonable conclusions. That may not be "knowledge" and it certainly isn't "absolute," but it isn't ignorance, either.

RICK: Oh, so you admit we can't know about these things?

NINA: What I think is that apartheid (to take our previous example) is *either* right *or* wrong: it cannot be both, regardless of where and when it is practiced. If the stronger argument suggests that it is wrong (as it seems to me it does) then I think it reasonable to conclude that it *is* wrong—unless or until we can come up with new arguments one way or the other. It's as though there is an absolute right and wrong, but we can't know it absolutely!

RICK: If we can't say for sure what it is, then why bother about it at all? Why not just talk about what people think is right or wrong?

NINA: I have no problem with that—no one can say that he or she knows with any certainty what is right or what is wrong. But you must admit that what some people think is sometimes more reasonable than what other people think. And the more reasonable position is more likely to be the "correct" position in some sense. But this needn't lead to dogmatism and intolerance, since the process is left open to new arguments and new evidence.

RICK: That's another thing that bugs me.

NINA: What?

RICK: Your preoccupation with what is "reasonable." Why do you make such a big deal out of this anyway? Why should we prefer reasonable positions to unreasonable ones? Sometimes its a good thing to cut loose and do what everyone else calls "unreasonable." What about feelings? Where do they fit in your scheme? How can you exclude feelings from ethics, anyway?

NINA: I don't exclude feelings. I don't see how anyone could think about something like apartheid and *not* have strong feelings about it! I'm just not sure what to say about them. For me they're a good place to start, but I'm not sure we can rely on feelings altogether: I don't think we can say apartheid is wrong just because I have strong feelings of antipathy toward it.

RICK: Why not?

NINA: Because I might just as easily *not* have those strong feelings, or, worse yet, I could have strong feelings in *favor* of apartheid! And yet it still seems to me reasonable to insist that apartheid is ethically wrong—regardless of our feelings.

RICK: There you go again! Who's to say it's reasonable? To me it is perfectly reasonable to say that apartheid is right for those who do not feel antipathy and wrong for those who do.

NINA: Then there's no real disagreement? Just different feelings?

RICK: Exactly!

NINA: And, I gather, if a person doesn't feel anything one way or the other, apartheid is neither right nor wrong?

RICK: Sure. Why not?

NINA: But what about those of us who try to provide some basis for our claims, some sort of evidence and argument, over and above any feelings we might have?

RICK: So what? People like you *feel* that an argument is required, so you muster one up.

NINA: So there's no such thing as a weak or a strong argument, just arguments and the way we feel about them?

RICK: Well, I'm not so sure in general. But in ethics it may be so.

NINA: What do you do about the fact that occasionally (at least) an argument or evidence can change the way we feel about something—even in ethics? What do you do about the fact that you can have strong feelings that something is wrong and yet an argument can persuade you that it's right despite your conflicting feelings?

RICK: What do you have in mind?

NINA: Well, homosexuality for example. I know you have strong feelings of disgust about homosexuality and yet you cannot provide any arguments to support that view. I might even be able to present you with a strong argument to convince you that homosexuality is not immoral or unethical and you might have to agree—regardless of how you *feel* about it.

RICK: So?

NINA: So . . . the argument is not simply something we attach willy-nilly to feelings; arguments and feelings can function independently of one another. There can be strong arguments in support of positions we feel deeply are wrong. And if the argument is strong, that is, we cannot find any way to weaken it, we must accept its conclusion regardless of how we feel. If there is a strong argument in support of a practice such as homosexuality, and if someone still feels that it's wrong, but can't show why, then he or she is probably mistaken. Moving the issue to the level of argument and evidence and removing it from the level of personal feelings allows us to consider ethical conflict as an arena of genuine agreement and disagreement, and requires that we continue to search for reasonable positions and abandon unreasonable ones— regardless of how we feel. It allows us to resolve ethical conflict, reasonably.

RICK: Well perhaps so. It all sounds like a lot of trouble. But I still worry about your idea of what's "reasonable." We could take any six people at random and get six different definitions of what that word means. In addition, I doubt whether any one of them would recognize it if they saw it!

NINA: You're probably right about that—at least as far as "reasonableness" is concerned. But they would have less trouble recognizing what is "unreasonable"! That's why we look for,

CALVIN AND HOBBES © 1991, *Universal Press Syndicate.*

and reject, unreasonable positions in ethics. Incoherence, inconsistency, contradiction, and downright factual inaccuracy are pretty easy to spot. We can even spot unreasonable prejudices. After we have rejected a claim as "unreasonable" we can suppose that the claims that are left, which we have no grounds to reject, are reasonable. But that's hardly dogmatic or intolerant. The process is always open to correction and modification and we're never sure we have reached "the truth." The only thing we insist upon is that there *is* a "truth" and we seek to apprehend it *by degrees* through the process of critical thinking.

CHAPTER THREE

DEVISING A PROCEDURE

1: CRITICAL THINKING SKILLS

We have stressed the fact that relative claims differ from nonrelative claims because of the type of support (or lack of support) the different claims have. What this means is that when ethical conflicts arise, attention should shift from the claims themselves ("Brutus shouldn't have killed Caesar") to the support for those claims. That support can be in the form of other claims ("Brutus miscalculated Caesar's ambition. Furthermore, the Republic became an Empire under Caesar's nephew Octavian in spite of Caesar's death.") or in the way the claims go together to make an argument.

In this context, the word "argument" does not mean what it means when your cousin Dudley and his buddy Al argue over whether the Celtics will take the NBA this year. That is, it does not involve shouting and throwing half-empty beer cans at one another, though if Dudley and Al ever calm down they might offer reasons *why* the Celtics will (or will not) take the NBA this year. In this book, supporting a conclusion with reasons constitutes an "argument."

The Argument Structure

It is important that we learn how to construct and dismantle arguments and what it is that makes them good (strong) or bad (weak). An argument always has a point to make, called the "conclusion." In thinking about an argument the first thing we must do is determine (1) whether or not it *is* an argument and, if it is, (2) what the conclusion is. All of the steps in the argument link together in a chain or web to support the conclusion. These steps are called "premises" or, simply, "reasons." Usually the conclusion is identified by an indicator term, such as "therefore," or "thus." We also frequently use indicator terms that suggest reasons rather than conclusions, indicators such as "because" or "since." The most common indicator terms are the following:

Conclusions	*Reasons*
therefore	because
thus	since
it follows that	as
consequently	for
hence	in view of the fact that
which means that	given that
so	inasmuch as

Unfortunately, when arguments are put forward, sometimes there are no indicators at all, making our job more complicated. In addition, indicators such as "since" may not be logical connectors at all, because "since" can refer to *time* as in "I've been here since 3:00 P.M. yesterday afternoon." We must decide when we see the indicators whether or not there is a logical connection (as there was in the previous sentence when we used the word "because") and even if we do not see any indicators we must still determine whether there is a logical connection. In other words, if we suspect that an argument might be present, we must look for logical connections between the statements: if we find indicators, fine; if not, we must decide whether the connections are there anyway. The easiest way to do this is to insert a reliable indicator where we think one belongs (such as "therefore" or "because") and see whether or not it changes the meaning of the passage in which we suspect there might be an argument. Let us take a couple of easy examples to clarify this important point.

EXAMPLE #1

The Celtics will take the NBA again this year, because Larry Bird is back and healthy and they finally have a good big man in the middle to help out Robert Parrish. In addition, the Supersonics got burned in the draft, Detroit may lose Isaiah, Jordan has a knee injury that may require surgery, and Magic Johnson has retired.

Analysis

This is an argument containing the reliable indicator "because" that points to the latter portions of this passage as the reasons or support for the conclusion, which is that "the Celtics will take the NBA again this year." We haven't asked whether or not this is a strong or "good" argument yet; we must determine first whether it is an argument at all. It is. Note that the word "because" could have been left out and it still would be an argument. That is, if we had said that "the Celtics will take the NBA again this year. Larry Bird is back, . . ." we could insert the indicator "because" and we could see the logical connection that exists between the first statement (the conclusion) and the rest of the passage (the reasons). The important thing to note is that there *is* a logical connection between the reasons and the conclusion. Take another passage where there is no such connection.

EXAMPLE #2

The Celtics will take the NBA again this year. Your cousin Dudley is a big Celtics fan, the Timberwolves got a new mascot this season who looks like Rin Tin Tin, and the Laker cheerleaders are getting new costumes.

Analysis

There are no indicators here. Furthermore, if we put one between the two sentences we change things considerably, imposing a different meaning on the passage. There simply is no connection between these statements. This passage is an example of what is called "exposition," and it differs from argument in that the statements are disconnected and there is no point, or conclusion, to the passage.

The "WHY?" Question

If we are not sure whether there is an argument in a given passage, one reliable test is to ask "the why? question." If statements are connected together logically, asking "why?" after any given statement that *seems* to be the conclusion will help us determine whether or not it is, in fact. Psychologically speaking, arguments are directional: they lead our minds from premises to conclusions. Asking "why?" after what seems to be the conclusion will direct us toward reasons when they are present. Take another example.

EXAMPLE #3

The Vikings are riddled with dissension and have no team unity. The Packers and Tampa Bay are at least a year away as yet, and the Lions are the only other team in the Division to pose any threat. But they don't match up well with the Bears. The Bears will dominate the Central Division again this year.

Analysis

As you read this, you might suspect that the final statement is the conclusion. All the statements appear to be connected and there also seems to be a direction toward that final statement. Put that claim first, and then ask "why?" and see what happens:

"The Bears will dominate the Central Division again this year." WHY? "Because the Vikings are riddled. . . . (etc.)" We have an argument, it has a conclusion, and there are reasons that support the conclusion. Insertion of the indicator "because" doesn't change the meaning of this passage, it simply makes it clear that an argument is present. Contrast this with example #2 and note how asking the "why?" question in the earlier example would not have directed your mind toward either the first or the second statement. That is because in that example the statements have no logical connection with one another.

REMEMBER: Look for indicators. They will help you find the

conclusion if there is one. Ask the "why?" question if you suspect there is a conclusion, and try inserting indicators where you think they should be. If you think you have located the conclusion, insert a reliable indicator (such as "because" following a conclusion or "therefore" preceding a conclusion) and see whether the passage has retained its meaning or changed somehow. If you simply do not see any connection between any of the statements and no one statement seems to stand out as the conclusion of the passage, you probably are not dealing with an argument. Your common sense is a fairly reliable guide, but careful reading is essential.

Evaluating Arguments

If you are dealing with an argument and you have located the conclusion you are halfway there! The next step is to determine whether or not the argument is strong. The strength of the argument is determined by asking two fundamental questions: (1) Is the support factually correct or at least plausible? (2) How close is the connection between the reasons, or premises, and the conclusion? Let us take the first item.

For testing the plausibility of reasons, the most reliable method is that of "counter-examples." If, for example, I insist that affirmative action programs invariably lead to hiring quotas and are therefore discriminatory, you might counter with examples of such programs that have *not* led to discrimination in the past. Such counter-examples will weaken my claim that is supposed to support my conclusion and thus weaken the argument as a whole. The more counter-examples we can provide, the less plausible the claim becomes and, therefore, the weaker the argument.

We can also counter support claims by simply refuting those claims that purport to be factual. If, for example, a member of the Ku Klux Klan were to insist that blacks are inferior to whites because they are less intelligent as a result of a smaller cranial capacity, we could counter by showing that "inferiority" is not a function of intelligence, that there is no logical connection between cranial capacity and intelligence, and/or that blacks do not (in fact) have a smaller cranial capacity than whites.

We should note that even when we cannot verify or falsify the truth of a claim given as a reason in support of an argument, strictly speaking, we can still ask whether or not it is a "good" reason, that is, whether or not it is *plausible* in the context of the argument. This process is called "weighing reasons" to determine whether or not they support the conclusion. The same process is employed in ethical decision-making to determine which of two or three choices seems to be the right thing to do. The trick is to reject those reasons that require further support, or those reasons that are incoherent or inconsistent with what we generally accept as true (they just "don't fit"), and to look for those that remain after the critical process has been completed. Two things are important in this process: (1) Keep a critical attitude (while remaining open-minded). (2) Ask good questions!

Connecting Premises with Conclusions

The techniques for scrutinizing the connection between premises and conclusions are a bit more complicated than simply adopting a critical attitude and asking good questions. They require that we determine whether there is a "gap" between the reasons given and the conclusion that purportedly rests on those reasons. In a strong argument the premises are true (or plausible) and there is little, if any, gap between premises and the conclusion. The absence of a gap between premises and conclusions signals what logicians call "strict entailment": if we accept the premises we *must* accept the conclusion as stated whether we want to or not! If there is a gap between premises and the conclusion, entailment is "loose"—or there is none at all. The wider the gap the looser the entailment, until it gets so wide there is no entailment between premises and conclusion at all!

The word "gap" is a metaphor suggesting that in the case of loose entailment it is possible to reject the conclusion even if we accept the premises—we might even draw *another* conclusion. As we mentioned above, arguments are directional: they lead our minds from the reasons to the conclusion. If there is a gap between the reasons and the conclusion, we can change directions and go to another conclusion.

Argument Chains: Strict Entailment

In arguments that exhibit strict entailment, premises are linked together in such a way that the conclusion becomes another link in what is an intellectual chain, but one that is only as strong as the weakest link. What this means is that if any one of the premises can be shown to be false, the entire chain, including the conclusion, is weakened. If the weak link, or premise, cannot be strengthened by further argument support or new factual evidence, the argument as a whole fails. We can see this by means of a simple example:

EXAMPLE #4

(1) Socrates was a man.
(2) All men are mortal.
(3) Therefore, Socrates was mortal.

This is a classical case of strict entailment. The premises (sentences #1 and #2) are linked together (by means of the common term "man") to support the conclusion (#3). If we grant that the premises are true, the conclusion necessarily follows, and we have no choice but to accept it. However, if one of the premises were false—let us say historians prove that Socrates never lived—the entire argument would break down. If we can break one link (premise) in the chain, the entire chain (argument) is destroyed.

Argument Webs: Loose Entailment

Most of the conclusions we try to reach are not strictly entailed by premises we can say are true; they are *loosely* entailed by those premises and are more or less plausible as the premises are more or less likely to be true. That is, there is almost always some gap between premises and conclusions. Such arguments can *still* be good arguments, however. Arguments involving loose entailment between reasons and the conclusion are strong if their premises are true (or plausible) and the gap is narrow between those premises and the conclusion they support. In such cases the conclusion is likely to be true, even though it is not certain. Generally, the wider the gap between premises and conclusions, the weaker the argument.

The point has been well put by David Kelly in his excellent logic book, *The Art of Reasoning*. Kelly tells us that

> [w]e assess strength by seeing how much free play there is between premises and conclusion. The technique is to assume that the premises are true, and then ask whether there could still be a reasonable doubt as to whether the conclusion is true. Assuming that the premises are true, is the stated conclusion the only one consistent with the evidence they provide? In that case the argument is strong. Or are there other conclusions that would be equally consistent with the evidence? In that case the argument is weaker.[1]

If we can say that the premises of an argument involving strict entailment are linked together to form a chain, we might say that the premises of an argument that involves loose entailment form the strands of a spider web—to borrow a metaphor from Kelly. The more strands of the web there are, the stronger the argument becomes—even though we do not find strict entailment here. We can weaken the argument by attacking and breaking down one strand, or premise, but we do not thereby destroy the argument as a whole. Let us take another example:

EXAMPLE #5

(1) Harry is hard of hearing, and (2) has poor vision. He (3) has had three speeding tickets in the past two months, (4) several minor accidents, and (5) one major accident in the same time period. I say, then, that (6) Harry is a poor driver.

Notice the lack of common terms in the premises, which have no logical connection with one another. Rather, they are simply a series of separate and independent considerations that converge on a conclusion that is *supported* by the premises, but not strictly *entailed* by them. The conclusion is likely to be true if the premises are true, but we could accept all of the premises and the conclusion might still be false (Harry might have attended driving school since these incidents—or, perhaps he stopped drinking!). Furthermore, we could show any premise to be false (Harry has 20/20 vision, let us say) and yet the argument is still fairly strong. The argument does not fall apart the way the chain argument in example #4 does. There are plenty of *other* reasons why Harry should lose his license!

Consider Both Entailment and Plausibility

Whether or not we find ourselves dealing with premises that are connected like links in a chain or like strands in a spider web, the argument strength depends upon the truth or plausibility of those premises and the way the premises are connected to the conclusion. In the rare cases when conclusions are strictly entailed by their premises, the argument collapses if one premise is shown to be false; in the more common arguments in which conclusions are more loosely connected to their premises, the argument is weakened, but not destroyed, if a premise is shown to be false.

We should note that entailment is a purely *formal* relationship between premises (reasons) and conclusions. By itself it cannot dictate that an argument is strong, because arguments can still be weak even though the conclusion is strictly entailed by the premises. As we have said, the strength of an argument is a function of *both* entailment and the truth of the premises: if the premises are not true—or even if one premise is not true—the argument is weakened. On the other hand, even if the premises are true, if there is a gap between the premises and the conclusion (if there is no entailment) the argument is also weak. Consider examples #6 and #7 in this regard.

EXAMPLE #6

All short men are insecure, and since Fred is a short man, he must be insecure.

As in the case of example #4, the conclusion of this argument is strictly entailed by the premises indicated by the words "and since." If we accept the premises, we *must* accept the conclusion, which is necessary, given the truth of the premises. However, we do not accept the premises as true. Clearly, the first premise, "All short men are insecure" is false; it comprises the weak link in this chain and destroys the argument. Not only must the conclusion be supported by the premises, but the premises stated must also be true, or at least plausible.

Another example will illustrate the contrary condition. With true premises but no entailment the argument also fails.

EXAMPLE #7

Harry has poor hearing and weak eyes. Further, he has received several speeding tickets in the past couple of months, during which time he has also had several traffic accidents. Therefore, Harry is a rotten husband.

The premises may be true, but the conclusion does not follow from those premises. There is no entailment here whatever—just a large gap between the premises and the conclusion. Indeed, we should draw a totally *different* conclusion, the signal that we are dealing with a very weak argument. The reasonable conclusion to draw from these premises is that Harry is a poor driver—not that he is a rotten husband!

The paradigm case of a strong argument, then, is one in which the conclusion is strictly entailed by the premises given and those premises are true, or very likely to be true.

Suppressed Premises

As if things were not complicated enough, we quite often encounter arguments with suppressed or missing premises. As critical thinkers we must discover what those missing premises are and place them in the argument where they belong. Although the person advancing the argument has primary responsibility for making it as strong as possible, it is also our responsibility—in accordance with what is sometimes called "the principle of charity"—to give the argument the benefit of every doubt. This sometimes means helping complete an incomplete argument.

If you recall the analogy with the chain, the weak link is often found in the missing premise, or unstated assumption, that is supposed to hold the argument together. It is important, therefore, that we know how to find these assumptions and make them explicit so that we can examine the argument and determine whether we should accept the position it advances.

When an argument fails to include a step or a reason, that is, when an assumption is being made, we need to ask ourselves what *else* must we know, besides what is given, to allow us to grant that particular conclusion? That "something else" is frequently the assumption. Take another example.

EXAMPLE #8

Rudy can't possibly be a levelheaded person under stress. He's a redhead.

Analysis

There is an argument here, believe it or not! When we ask the "why?" question, it leads us to the first statement as the conclusion and the second as a reason. We can then insert an indicator term, as follows:

"Rudy can't possibly be a levelheaded person under stress, because he's a redhead."

Clearly, though, there is something missing. Ask yourself: what *else* must I know to grant the conclusion? The answer can be found by looking for a term that appears in the conclusion but nowhere else in the argument. The assumption will have something to do with that term. As a rule, in any argument if a term appears in the conclusion but nowhere else in the argument, an assumption has been made. In this case, the missing premise will have something to do with being levelheaded under stress, because that term suddenly appears in the conclusion and nowhere in the premises. We need to find out what is assumed to be generally true about this quality. The answer is the claim, that "redheads are not levelheaded persons under stress." Now as it happens this is a very weak claim, and it is a very weak link in this argument as well. We can set it up as follows:

"Rudy can't possibly be a levelheaded person under stress because he's a redhead, and redheads are not levelheaded persons under stress." In this argument the conclusion is strictly entailed by the premises, but one of the premises states a false claim. The argument is therefore unacceptable.

Illustrations

Let us take some more examples, working from weaker arguments to stronger arguments in order to see how to determine which are which.

EXAMPLE #9

REPORTER: Senator, would you please explain why you voted for the B-1 bomber, especially in light of the cost overruns and the widespread criticism of that particular plane?

SENATOR: Certainly. I will be glad to. It is imperative that we have a safe and secure defense system, that we keep America strong and our enemies weak. The surest way to squander our precious heritage is to knuckle under to our enemies abroad and peace can only be guaranteed by a strong defense.

Analysis

If we say that the Senator's conclusion is that America's defenses must be strong and we assume along with him that the B-1 is necessary to maintain that strength (which is doubtful), there is still little, if any, connection between the reasons he gives and the conclusion he wants to draw. That is, even if we accepted the reasons the Senator gives, we might still refuse to accept the conclusion as true—there is a gap between the reasons and the conclusion! Indeed, a different conclusion altogether might be said to follow from those same premises. Can you determine what it might be? Consider, furthermore, whether or not we would be "knuckling under" to our "enemies" by cutting back on our defense spending. Why should we accept this as true? It is certainly not self-evident, and the Senator gives no support for this claim. An important issue being ignored here is whether or not our present defenses can adequately deter the "enemy" and ensure peace. Peace may not require more military spending. But even if it does, it is not clear why the B-1 must be part of that spending. There are several problems here, and the argument's tendency to wither under scrutiny suggests that it is rather weak. A stronger argument would not invite so many questions and doubts about its premises, and it would have a tighter connection between the premises and its conclusion. Take another example.

Example #10

"The fact that a majority of the States, reflecting after all the majority sentiment in those States, have had restrictions on abortions for at least a century seems to me as strong an indication as there is that the asserted right to an abortion is not 'so rooted in the traditions and conscience of our people as to be ranked fundamental.' " [*Roe v Wade*, J. Rehnquist, dissenting]

Analysis

This argument is fairly strong, certainly stronger than the previous one. If we accept the premises we are bound to accept the conclusion that is supported by those premises, and which is unstated but obvious from the position Rehnquist takes on this issue. If we stated it, we might put it this way: "therefore, I do not consider abortion a fundamental human right." But the first statement is questionable: why accept the claim that *because* States "have had restrictions on abortions for at least a century" *therefore* the sentiment in those States is in opposition to abortion? What sort of restrictions do those States have? How can we be sure that the laws in those States reflect majority sentiment? How old are the laws restricting abortions in those States? Even though they might have reflected majority sentiment at one time, can we say they still do? We can see that there are a number of important questions that must be answered before we can grant the truth of this premise. Thus, even though there is strict entailment between the reasons stated and the conclusion we imagined to follow from those reasons, the conclusion must remain in doubt until we can establish stronger plausibility for the first premise—either by way of further evidence or argument. An even stronger argument follows:

Example #11

Certain chemicals are known to cause cancer in laboratory animals, and when this happens there is a likelihood that these same chemicals will cause cancer in humans. It would seem prudent, therefore, to avoid these chemicals whenever possible.

Analysis

This is a strong argument. The conclusion is entailed by the premises given and the premises appear to be true, though there is a missing premise to the effect that it is prudent to avoid chemicals that cause cancer. Presumably, the author of this argument thought this was self-evident. Note here that the plausibility of the premises is increased by use of such terms and phrases as "there is a liklihood" and "it would seem prudent." When claims are modified by such qualifiers they are stronger than if they are asserted universally by means of such terms as "always" or "never," "all," or "none." We can apply this to the example of hotheaded redheads. It is easier to support the claim that "some" or perhaps even "many" redheads have hot tempers than it is to support the claim that they *all* do! This is a good thing to remember when we consider arguments and when we try to put our own arguments together: *we strengthen our arguments by making our claims more modest and we weaken them by making broad, sweeping claims that are hard to support.*

* * *

We have seen what a strong argument is and how strong arguments differ from weak ones. We have also learned to "weigh" reasons when we cannot determine with confidence that they are true or false: those reasons are "good reasons" that are more resistant to criticism; those reasons that cannot withstand critical scrutiny are bad reasons or no reasons at all. The purpose of criticism in the process of ethical reasoning is, therefore, a positive one: to formulate the best arguments we can to support the ethical positions we take and to recognize the most reasonable of several options when we are faced with difficult choices.

2. TRAPS AND PITFALLS: INFORMAL FALLACIES

The mistakes in reasoning that all of us make daily are referred to as "informal fallacies," in contrast to violations of the formal rules of logic. Arguments that commit informal fallacies are weak because they result in a lack of entailment between the premises and

the conclusion. The weakness in an argument caused by an informal fallacy is internal to the argument and has nothing to do with
whether the conclusion is true or false: it is simply not true or false
for the reasons given.

There are over one hundred informal fallacies, but we shall look
at only a few of the most common ones that arise in ethical
reasoning, fallacies that comprise traps and pitfalls to good ethical
arguments. We shall consider the following four fallacies: illicit
appeal to authority, red herring, bifurcation, and appeal to emotion.

Illicit Appeal to Authority

As a rule, there is nothing "illicit" about an appeal to authority.
Indeed, if we could not appeal to authority to establish many of our
truth claims, we would be able to make very few claims at all. But
some of these appeals are legitimate while others are not. Thus, if
my physics book tells me that the temperature on Mars is extremely cold at night, I can claim to "know" that fact on good
authority. If, on the other hand, Mr. Spock makes the same claim
on an episode of *Star Trek*, and I insist that it is true *because* Spock
says it is true, the knowledge claim is bogus: the claim lacks
support. The key here is the legitimacy of the appeal to authority
and the relevance of that person's testimony to the issue at hand.
Claims are more or less probable depending on whether or not the
authority we appeal to is a legitimate authority on the question at
issue. An "illicit appeal" is an appeal to an authority who happens
to be outside his or her range of expertise. When it comes to
questions of acting in a TV series, for example, Leonard Nimoy
(who plays Mr. Spock) has some legitimacy as an authority. If we
wanted to establish the claim that acting in a TV series is more
demanding on the actor than, say, making a movie—because
Nimoy says so—the argument would have some initial plausibility. In the case of the Doonesbury cartoon in this section, the
illicit nature of Pat Robertson's appeal has to do with the question
of whether there *are* such things as "celestial insiders," and if so
whether Mr. Robertson can be supposed to have privileged access
to their advice. But this is a special case of the illicit appeal to
authority!

The candidate for President here (Pat Robertson) commits what may be the ultimate appeal to illicit authority! Even though the credentials of the authority are unimpeachable, the appeal to that authority is itself questionable—at the least! DOONESBURY © 1992 by G. B. Trudeau. Reprinted with permission of Universal Press Syndicate. All rights reserved.

Strictly speaking, any appeal to authority raises some doubts: nothing is true simply because somebody says it is true. But, at the same time, some appeals to authority are more legitimate than others. To avoid the fallacy of illicit appeal to authority, one must consider the credentials of the authority appealed to in support of the conclusion, as well as the question of the reliability of the claim made by that authority.

One good rule of thumb in areas in which we feel out of our element (because the questions are too technical or we have no basis for establishing or rejecting credentials) is to ask whether the authority appealed to has any particular axe to grind: an authority that has an axe to grind is likely to be less reliable than one who does not. A spokesperson for Exxon who says that an oil spill does not endanger the wildlife in the area is less likely to be a reliable authority than a biologist at a nearby university who has no particular job interest in the truth or falsity of his claims.

Appeal to Emotion

If I argue that Steve Jones cannot possibly be a murderer because he has such an innocent face, I commit the fallacy of appeal to emotion—pity in this case. There is no logical connection whatever between having an innocent face and having an inclination to murder. As we saw in the last section, we could accept the premise

(Jones has an innocent face) and draw any number of possible conclusions: (1) His parents must be good-looking people; (2) He must have broken a lot of hearts as a young man; (3) He is guilty as sin: no one can be that innocent. But if in a court of law a clever defense counselor points to his client's face with its innocent expression we might very well, as members of the jury, find ourselves moved by that expression to draw the conclusion that the defendant is not guilty—despite the evidence to the contrary. We can also be moved by fear, patriotism, sex appeal, or appeal to large numbers (which is especially common in ethical reasoning, when we say that something must be right because "everyone" does it).

We should be wary of conclusions claimed *simply because* of assorted appeals to emotions that have no logical bearing whatever on those conclusions. Whether or not "everyone" does something has nothing to do with the question of whether or not it would be right to do that thing, no matter how much we *want* to be just like everyone else! Having an innocent face (whatever that means) has nothing whatever to do with the question of guilt or innocence in a murder trial.

During the Watergate scandal, just after Richard Nixon was reelected President, a standard defense of the actions of the Committee to Reelect The President in its burglaries and "dirty tricks" was that such things were "always" happening in politics: "everyone does it; why pick on Nixon?" This is a weak argument, of course, because we can accept the reasons given as true (which they may well be, with qualification) and still reject the conclusion. To be more specific: (Almost) every politician plays dirty tricks on

Unfortunately, J.J. commits the fallacy of "appeal to emotion" in this exchange.
DOONESBURY © 1992 by G. B. Trudeau. Reprinted with permission of
Universal Press Syndicate. All rights reserved.

the opposition. Therefore, this politician is justified in doing so.

Put in this bare-bones fashion, we can clearly see the gaps in the reasoning that mark this as a weak argument. It needs to be shown that what "almost everyone" does is justified. There is a gap here that needs to be filled by further argument. We need to bridge the gap between "what almost every politician" does and what is "justified." This argument's weakness is also evident from the fact that the conclusion stated is only one of several that could be drawn from the reason given, even if we grant that that reason is true.

Red Herring

In the "red herring" fallacy, a case is made for one conclusion and presented as though it were a case for another, sometimes unrelated, conclusion. Consider, for example, the Doonesbury cartoon below.

In this cartoon, Mark Slackmeyer, a disc jockey for NPR, is recounting the names of Reagan appointees "charged with legal or ethical misconduct." The cartoon is the sixth in a series of cartoons dealing with what Trudeau calls "Sleaze on Parade," and Larry Speakes has called Mark to counter his charges.

Speakes refers to the reading of the 103 names as a "vicious smear campaign by the liberal press." Now, whether or not we know what to call this allegation, we can quickly see that there is a flaw in Speakes' logic. Let us put his argument together to see how and where this flaw arises. In doing this we must do a little imaginative reconstructing, since a cartoon does not allow for a full-fledged argument—even supposing that readers demanded such things!

Speakes' argument appears to be as follows:

(R) Sleaze on Parade is a vicious smear campaign by the liberal press.

(C) Therefore, we should not condemn the 103 appointees who must be presumed "innocent" persons of "integrity."

An assumption is operating here, of course. It appears to be that (A) such smear campaigns by the "liberal press" slander innocent persons.

What is important for us to consider is that the central issue is the guilt or innocence of the 103 appointees whose names are being

DOONESBURY © 1992 by G. B. Trudeau. Reprinted with permission of
Universal Press Syndicate. All rights reserved.

read over the radio. The flaw in the logic of Speakes' counterargument is that it ignores that issue altogether and diverts attention to
another, unrelated issue: namely, the reliability of the "liberal
press." The red herring results from the fact that the premise stated
introduces an issue *irrelevant* to the main concern of whether those
persons are guilty of "legal and ethical misconduct" while in office.
More importantly, and this is where the term "red herring" arises,
the irrelevant issue purposely diverts attention from the central
issue. The press may or may not be "liberal," and it may or may not
slander innocent persons. But the 103 persons whose names are
read on the air may *still* be guilty as charged. That issue has not
been joined.

The same sort of fallacy is committed when someone like the
Senator in the last section argues for continued development of the
B-1 bomber on the grounds that opposition to such development is
opposition to "a strong national defense." When this phrase is
introduced into the debate, attention shifts from the issue of the
bomber to the unrelated issue of a strong national defense. (Note,
by the way, the emotional appeal in the phrase "strong national
defense." This is common in the red herring fallacy.) It isn't clear,
for example, that a strong national defense cannot be achieved by
means *other* than continued development of the B-1 bomber. One
could accept the reasons given (that we should have a strong
national defense) without accepting the conclusion that we should
continue to develop the B-1 bomber. Once again, a gap exists
between the premises and the conclusion: a number of possible
conclusions can be drawn from the reasons given, even if we allow

that the reasons are all true. This tells us that we are dealing with a weak argument: there is no entailment here. Indeed, there is a fallacy, a red herring!

Bifurcation (False Dichotomy)

The final fallacy we shall consider is a form of oversimplification that tends to reduce disjunctions to exclusive either/or statements without allowing for the possibility that there are other options.

Unless the two options she offers are the only ones possible, J.J. may be committing the fallacy of "bifurcation" in this exchange. DOONESBURY
© *1992 by G. B. Trudeau. Reprinted with permission of Universal Press Syndicate. All rights reserved.*

In a more serious vein, consider the following brief, typical argument over abortion:

"If you are in favor of abortion you are in favor of infanticide: you're either 'pro-choice' or 'pro-life'—there is no middle ground on this issue. Now I've heard you say many times that you're in favor of abortion. Therefore, you're advocating infanticide: you're in favor of the killing of innocent babies."

This is an example of oversimplification in the form of bifurcation, coupled with reliance upon a very vague catch term, "pro-life." It is not at all clear that everyone who opposes abortion is "pro-life." Nor is it clear that everyone who is "pro-choice" is *not* "pro-life." For example, one could be against abortion but in favor of war and the death penalty, or opposed to war and the death penalty but in favor of abortion in certain instances. The term "pro-life" is a misnomer in these cases. Additionally, many who approve of abortion on demand deny that the fetus is an infant and would object to the term "infanticide" and consider it a form of begging the question—another informal fallacy that arises when one assumes what is yet to be proven, in this case that the fetus is an infant and that abortion is therefore murder.

The bifurcation appears clearly in the phrase "you're either 'pro-choice' or 'pro-life'—there is no middle ground on this issue." Ruling out the middle ground, or third or fourth alternatives, reduces the disjunction "either/or" to *exclusive* terms and does not allow for shades of gray. In the "real world," as they say, shades of gray abound and we must beware the tendency to disallow this middle ground—which may be the reasonable ground to take.

We need to guard against the use of fallacious reasoning ourselves and to be wary of it when used by others as well. Fallacies, informal though they are, weaken the connection between reasons, or premises, and conclusions.

A Suggested Procedure

Before leaving our present discussion let's make sure we have a specific plan for evaluating arguments. Let's consider a procedure that will work in considering any argument as we look for weaknesses and try to strengthen our ethical reasoning.

Remember to use this technique in criticizing your own arguments as well as those of others. The purpose of this technique is to find statements and connections among statements that can withstand criticism and which seem, therefore, to be true. As we say this, we would urge a word of caution: beware of half-truths!

Some of the most troublesome claims to verify are those that are neither obviously true nor obviously false—they are a bit of both. If I say, for example, that "Caesar crossed the Rubicon," and the historical data support that claim, we can insist the claim is true. On the other hand, if I say that "Caesar did not cross the Rubicon," and the evidence flies in the face of that claim, then the claim is obviously false. If, however, I say that "When Caesar crossed the Rubicon it meant the end of the Roman Republic and the beginning of the Roman Empire," I have stated a half-truth. Portions of the claim (which is a compound statement) are historically accurate—Caesar did cross the Rubicon and the Republic was

PROCEDURE

1. **Locate key terms and clarify them if necessary.** We haven't discussed this, but it is an extremely important first step in analyzing any argument. It is not necessary (or possible) to clarify the meaning of every term in an argument, but it is necessary to be sure we know what the key terms mean so we're all operating "on the same page," so to speak.

2. **Find the main conclusion: What's the Point?** This is usually, but as we saw above not always, suggested by indicator terms. Ask the "why?" question.

3. **Look for argument support.** What reasons are given to support the conclusion? Simplify these reasons somewhat (without oversimplifying them) and eliminate any irrelevant premises. You can tell they are irrelevant if they do not affect the conclusion one way or the other. That is, even if an irrelevant reason is true, it makes no difference to the argument.

4. **Look for fallacies.** We have considered several common fallacies in this section.

5. **Evaluate the argument: Try to falsify.** Examine the claims that comprise the reasons and ask whether they are plausible. Use your common sense. Try to think of counter-examples and exceptions to the statements that support arguments. Are the reasons consistent and coherent among themselves? Consider the relation between the reasons given and the conclusion said to follow from those reasons. Look for entailment or the lack of entailment. Ask yourself, "If this is true does that follow?" or "If I accept this claim, must I accept the conclusion? (whether I want to or not!)" Good questions are the basis of good criticism.

6. **What's left? Where do we stand?** This is the heart of the method of critical thinking that we have mentioned throughout. What remains after thorough criticism is more likely to be true than what we start with.

replaced by the Empire. What is not at all clear is the implication contained in the statement that one event was the cause of the other. Indeed, it is not at all clear how we could establish causality in this case.

What we are saying, then, is this: watch out for compound claims that combine simple statements. Even though the simple statements may be true (as they are in the example just cited), the *connection* may be highly dubious. Also, watch out for broad, sweeping claims that cannot possibly be verified. For example, how would one even begin to verify the following types of claims?

• Magic Johnson was the greatest point guard who ever played the game!

• *Hamlet* is the most tragic play ever written.

• Caesar was one of the two or three most ambitious men who ever lived.

It is wise, as a general rule, to restrict ourselves to simple, modest claims for which evidence can provide a reasonable basis for informed consent or dissent. It is easier, as we noted in the text, to verify a modest claim ("Some redheads are bad-tempered") than it is grand, unqualified generalizations ("All short men have an attitude problem").

In a word: reject palpable falsehoods and embrace obvious truths, while guarding against half-truths and claims whose appeal is largely visceral.

* * *

We are now ready to return to the problems involved in specifically *ethical* reasoning. You may recall that our chief concern in the domain of ethics is to avoid relativism and to assure ourselves that our ethical conclusions are justified by the reasons and evidence we provide for them.

CHAPTER FOUR

THE JUSTIFICATION
OF ETHICAL CLAIMS

We turn now to the issue of justifying ethical claims, an issue that lies at the heart of ethical argument. When we are trying to resolve ethical conflict or determine which of several options is the right thing to do, we need to justify our decision by supporting it with cogent (strong) arguments, arguments that involve both accurate information and sound ethical principles.

1. WHAT JUSTIFICATION IS AND WHAT IT IS NOT

Two pretenders are sometimes confused with justification because they appear to involve the same procedures as justification. But they are not at all alike, and we can have a much better idea of what justification involves if we begin by understanding its look-alikes: rationalization and explanation.

Explanation Contrasted with Justification

Both justification and explanation seek to provide reasons why something is the case. We might try to justify having lied to our neighbor when she asked us whether or not we liked her ugly new hat, for example, or we might try to explain how the lie came about. In either case we give reasons, except that in the case of justification the reasons are supposed to support the claim that *one did the right thing* to lie. In the case of an explanation, on the other hand, we are trying to understand something we already know to be the case—the reasons we give increase our understanding; they do not support a conclusion that fails without that support. If one cannot justify having lied in the case of our example that is because the reasons given are not good reasons.

"Good Reasons" In Ethics

Good ethical reasons, generally, are relevant factual considerations (such as the fact that if we tell our neighbor the truth it will probably hurt her feelings) and normative claims that we find ourselves bound to accept *whether we want to or not*, and which make it possible for us to resolve ethical conflict reasonably. A normative claim is a claim that presupposes a "norm" or standard, such as an ethical principle. Normative claims contrast with "descriptive" claims that, when true, we call "facts." We noted this distinction in the second chapter. These claims comprise "good reasons" in ethics if they can withstand critical scrutiny and if they make the resolution of ethical conflict possible.

Of major concern to the nonrelativist in trying to make his case against the relativist are the ethical principles that must be incorporated into any attempt to justify ethical claims. We have already seen how difficult it is to establish these principles and demonstrate that they are free from cultural bias. In the end, it would seem, the best defense that can be made for any ethical principle is the success of that principle in helping us to resolve ethical conflict and make informed ethical choices.

The point we must insist upon is that rational principles are necessary for the possibility of the resolution of ethical conflict, and the viability of those principles is, ultimately, established by their success at resolving those conflicts ethically. It doesn't matter who put them forth or when or where. It doesn't matter how many people accept them or reject them. The only issue worth consideration is whether or not the principles allow for the possibility of a reasonable resolution to ethical conflict. If these principles allow us to resolve ethical conflict without acrimony and if they seem worthy of acceptance by other disinterested, rational persons, then for all practical purposes they are sound.

The three principles we put forward in the second chapter are just such principles. At that time, you will recall, we defended the first principle, concerning respect for persons, on the grounds that it is the cornerstone of any ethical system: ethics would not be possible without such a principle; it would reduce to whimsey or a struggle for power. To say, as we now do, that ethical principles are sound if they allow us to resolve ethical conflict reasonably is to say the same thing in other words. The test for these principles—all three of them—is to be found in the arena of ethical conflict and ethical decision-making. Despite the apparent circularity involved in such a test, it works well in the sciences in the form of the "hypothetico-deductive" method. And it also works in ethics.

Thus, we must include sound ethical principles along with pertinent factual information in the class of statements that provide good reasons in ethics.

How Do We Recognize "Bad" Ethical Reasons?

It might help us to get a firmer grasp of what count as "good reasons" in ethics by considering what do *not* count as good reasons. The American philosopher Ronald Dworkin has addressed the issue and argues that there are four types of reasons in ethics that "do not count" as good reasons. He mentions rationalization and prejudice, which we shall discuss more fully in a moment. To these two types he adds two more, "mere emotional reaction," and "parroting." Of the former he notes that

> We distinguish moral positions from emotional reactions, not because moral positions are supposed to be unemotional or dispassionate . . . but because the moral position is supposed to justify the emotional reaction, and not vice versa.[1]

"Parroting" is simply repeating what we have heard others say—usually without giving it any thought. The temptation simply to repeat what "everyone knows" is strong, but as we have seen it is also fallacious. Something is not necessarily true simply because a great many people think it is true. And something is not necessarily right simply because "everyone" does it.

Justification in ethics requires the mustering of good reasons and the avoidance of flawed reasoning and "bad" reasons to support our claims. In an explanation the reasons extend our grasp of a situation which is already known independently of those reasons. In rationalization, as we shall soon see, reasons are ultimately irrelevant—whether those reasons are good or bad.

We can explain why so many Southerners in the antebellum South owned slaves and became indignant when told they must relinquish that ownership. We can understand, further, how these people in many cases persuaded themselves that they were right to own slaves; how they rationalized by the use of bogus "scientific" information as "evidence" that because of a different cranial capacity blacks were inferior to whites and "therefore" deserving of their servitude. We can explain, and we can understand. But we cannot justify, because we cannot find any good, ethical reasons to support the claim that slave ownership is ethically right.

Rationalization Contrasted With Justification

The attempt to justify ownership of slaves in accordance with bogus "scientific evidence" is not a case of justification at all; rather, it is a case of rationalization. Rationalization, like justification, involves the giving of reasons to support a claim that something is right or proper. In the case of justification, the reasons do support the conclusion because the reasons are good reasons and the connection between the reasons and the conclusion is one of entailment. Rationalization, on the other hand, is a weak form of argument in which a conclusion is held *despite the fact* that reasons do not support that conclusion. The attempted justification of slave ownership can be seen to be thinly disguised rationalization, because it provides reasons for conclusions that are held independently of those reasons. We can reject all of the "scientific" evidence that "supports" the claim that slaves are deserving of their servitude and yet those who make those claims will probably maintain them anyway. Any conclusion based on rationalization is held on grounds of strong feelings and prejudice, not reason. The psychologist Gordon Allport argues that when prejudice is involved, rationalization consists in "the accommodation of beliefs to attitudes."[2] We modify and adapt loosely held generalizations (beliefs) to accommodate our feelings (attitudes) about people, events and ideas, when it would be wise to reason to more accurate generalizations and modify our attitudes accordingly.

We can see why rationalization is not like justification, even though the process sometimes appears to be the same. *The rejection of the reasons given in the process of rationalizing does not affect the conclusion in any way!*

Justification, on the other hand, is a process that depends on reasoning. Ethical claims take the form of conclusions. Conclusions, as we know, are only as strong as the reasons that support them, and the argument itself only as strong as the connections between reasons and conclusions. If we reject the reasons as false or implausible, or if the connection between the reasons and the conclusion is not one of entailment, we must reject the conclusion.

An Example of Rationalization Disguised As Justification

To see the difference more clearly, let us examine the reasoning involved in an example of attempted justification that clearly is a thinly disguised rationalization. This should help us get an even better understanding of the important differences between rationalization and justification.

In the *Minneapolis Tribune* on October 18, 1990 there appeared a photograph of a bespeckled man leaving a court house in Bangor, Maine with his daughter. The caption read as follows:

Hunter Acquitted of Manslaughter Charge.

Donald Rogerson and his daughter, Marcia, left Penobscot County Superior Court in Bangor, Maine, Wednesday after a jury found him not guilty of manslaughter in the November 1988 death of Karen Wood. Rogerson, 47, was hunting when he mistook Wood, 37, for a deer and shot her once in the chest behind her suburban home. The case pitted hunters against nonhunters in an emotional debate. Wood had moved from Iowa four months earlier with her husband and twin one-year-old daughters.

One of the jurors was quoted after the trial as saying (in effect) "She should have known better: there were hunters all over that area." Let us assume that this is that juror's "reason" for voting "not guilty" in this case. Unfortunately, it is not a "good reason." Among other things, it is not logically relevant to the conclusion. Consider:

(R) Wood shouldn't have been in her backyard with hunters all over the place.

(C) Therefore, Rogerson is not guilty of manslaughter.

There is no entailment whatever between this premise and the conclusion, as can be seen by the fact that the conclusion stated *or its contradictory* could be drawn with equal plausibility. The reason given might lead one to conclude that Karen Wood was careless, but it does not lead to the conclusion that Rogerson was not guilty of manslaughter. To say that he is not guilty of manslaughter is equivalent to saying that he didn't slay Karen Wood—which no one, including Rogerson himself, argues! There is simply no question that Rogerson was guilty of manslaughter. It was probably "involuntary" manslaughter, but it was manslaughter nonetheless. The jury's decision says, in effect, that Donald Rogerson did not kill Karen Wood, which is absurd!

A number of fascinating psychological and sociological reasons might well *explain* why the jurors voted as they did. Karen Wood and her family were "outsiders" in the Bangor community. Hunting is pursued by a large number of Maine residents and, more importantly, it brings in revenue from out-of-state hunters to a state that depends on the tourist trade. There may be other reasons as well, all of which would combine to explain why the jurors voted as they did. That is, knowing these things will allow us to grasp why these people felt as they did and why they might vote in such an irrational manner. It is even possible that we might sympathize with the jurors to the extent that we can say we would have voted the same way they did in those circumstances. But none of these reasons comprise good, philosophical reasons that would *justify* the claim that Donald Rogerson was not guilty of manslaughter.

It might be said that the juror quoted "had his reasons," and that he was able to "justify it to himself." But this is a misuse of the term "justify." One does not justify one's actions "to oneself." One justifies them to what has been called the "universal audience," which is an imaginary audience of disinterested, intelligent people who would feel compelled *by the force of the argument* to accept the conclusion put forward.[3] The jury's decision—being irrational—is unacceptable on rational grounds. That is, no reasonable person would accept it. The best that can be said about this reason for voting "not guilty" in the case of the death of Karen Wood is that it is an excellent example of "rationalization." It is an example of a reason given to support a conclusion held on nonrational grounds—as one suspects from the cryptic remark in the caption that "the case pitted hunters against nonhunters in an emotional debate." The argument cannot withstand criticism, since, even if the reason given is true (which is doubtful) it has no bearing whatever on the conclusion. It is therefore not a good, ethical reason.

Attempts to Justify the Opposite Point of View

Can we provide "good reasons" to justify the counterclaim, namely, the claim that the jury was *wrong* to have found Donald Rogerson not guilty? That is, can we put together an argument that counters the rationalization of the juror we quoted above that is not, itself, just another piece of rationalization? What we need are good reasons in the sense of that phrase noted above. We tried this earlier, you may recall, in the case of outlawing radar detectors. Can we do so in the case of hunters who shoot unwary housewives in their backyards? Surely, we can.

Donald Rogerson was guilty of involuntary manslaughter because he was careless in the use of his rifle and shot Karen Wood. Even though the killing of Karen Wood was involuntary, in that it was accidental, Rogerson still bears responsibility because he should have taken precautions (such as getting close enough to determine that Karen Wood was not a deer). In killing Wood, Rogerson violated her right to life, which is incorporated in our first principle, and what he did was therefore wrong.

This argument is simple and straightforward. It appears to be free of bias and evidences no rationalization or special pleading. It incorporates facts (Karen Wood was shot by Donald Rogerson), reasonable inferences (Rogerson was careless), and an ethical principle (Wood's right to life) that is entailed by our first principle, which we have argued is the cornerstone of ethics. Thus, the conclusion that the jury was wrong appears to be justified in this case. Can it withstand criticism?

Recall some of the things we have been maintaining in the book thus far: It is imperative in ethics if we are to avoid "relativism"— the reduction of all ethical claims to personal opinion or cultural bias—that we eliminate such bias when we find it creeping into our attempts to justify ethical claims. Furthermore, the reasons we give must be capable of sustaining rational scrutiny and compelling enough to warrant the consent of any disinterested bystander, that is, any member of the "universal audience." "Good reasons" are not simply reasons that persuade *me*, they are reasons that should persuade *anyone*.

The cultural relativist, of course, will deny that this is possible. He will say that "good reasons" are simply reasons accepted by members of a particular culture but not necessarily by members of another culture. The relativist, then, might not criticize the argument as we have given it here, but, rather, the attempt to justify *any* ethical claim. The relativist, you may recall, insists that the standards and principles of one culture cannot be "imposed" on another culture in the form of value judgments that arise within the former culture and are not recognized by the latter culture. Values and standards, it is said, are *relative to* particular cultures and cannot be employed to make "cross-cultural" value judgments. One might advance the following criticism: "We weren't there. We don't know what it was like. Who are we to say that the jury was wrong, anyway?"

Justification Is Not Culture-Bound

The heart of our response to this criticism is contained in Nina's responses to Rick in our dialogue and in the ensuing chapters of this book. Basically, it comes down to the insistence that our justification, as a *rational* justification, is not necessarily culture-bound. Rather than attempt to try to defend *this* claim, however, we would prefer to focus on examples and the attempts to provide justification that support (or fail to support) specific ethical claims. That is what we have done in the case of the radar detectors and in opposition to the members of the jury who found Donald Rogerson not guilty of manslaughter.

The juror in our example, or an owner of a radar detector, might not find our argument persuasive, however. But they *should*, because good reasons are culturally neutral and should appeal to any intelligent person who follows the argument and cannot find fault with the reasons given.

The focus of attention must always be on the reasoning process itself, and not the persons who put it forward or their cultural situation. The key question is not whether all, or only some, or any, people accept the reasons given. The key question is whether or not every person who hears the argument *should* accept it as sound—if for no other reason than there is no good reason not to do so.

Conflicting Ethical Claims Cannot Both Be Justified

In closing we should point out one rather important feature of justification: conflicting ethical claims cannot both be justified. If one claim conflicts with another, one or both of them must be false, and therefore incapable of being justified. Thus, for example, if the claim that "slavery is ethically wrong" can be justified, the conflicting claim that "slavery is not ethically wrong" *cannot* be justified. And vice versa. We may find it difficult to determine precisely how to justify one or the other of these claims, but after the attempt has been made one or the other of the supposed "justifications" must eventually fail. It is possible that they *both* will fail (because neither argument that supports the two claims can withstand criticism), but *they cannot both be successful.*

When it comes to conflicting ethical claims, then, there would appear to be three possibilities:

(1) Neither claim has any support in the way of factual information or argument and thus neither can be said to be justified. The only grounds for maintaining either claim, then, are personal grounds (feelings or intuitions) or cultural biases; the claims themselves are nothing more than personal or collective opinions.

(2) Both claims are supported by facts and arguments that cannot be dislodged by criticism. In this case neither claim is adequately justified and we must presume that more information or further discussion will lend support to one of the two conflicting claims at some future time. At the moment

we are at a "stand-off," and there is no *good reason* to embrace either claim. Thus, if we make a choice the grounds for this choice will be personal, as they were in #1. In the "real world," of course, we must make such choices from time to time even though neither option seems correct—or both seem equally correct. This does not mean that rational deliberation is fruitless, however. Rather, it simply means that there are limits to rational deliberation. Fortunately, the choices we make and the ethical claims we embrace in order to resolve conflict are often well supported and we are justified in saying what we say and doing what we do. Such is the third possibility.

(3) In this case one claim is supported by factual information and strong arguments, together with sound ethical principles, whereas the other is not. The former is, therefore, justified whereas the latter is not.

Consequently, when an ethical claim is made we should turn to the support for that claim and scrutinize it carefully, bearing in mind that faulty information or a weak connection between the reasons given and the claim itself weaken the argument as a whole. But even if the argument holds up under scrutiny, we must keep an open mind, because any reasoning process is corrigible and open to future correction. We can never be certain that we have "the truth" in ethics. But, clearly, everyone's opinion is not of equal merit, either.

Food for Further Thought

The key to the position put forward in these pages against relativism is the notion that "good reasons" appeal to anybody at any time; they are not "culture-bound." But is this possible? Is it possible to weigh reasons and assess them critically, as we have proposed in this book, *without* cultural considerations predominating? In other words, isn't it the case that our cultural bias is like a set of lenses through which we consider the reasons given to support ethical arguments: We are probably not even aware of them, but they color the way we hear and think about the reasons given. Because of this, what is "reasonable" in our culture is "unreasonable" in another.

There is considerable truth in this criticism. There can be no doubt that all of us, including the most dispassionate philosopher alive, is influenced by cultural factors. But "influence" does not entail "determine." We must beware of the fallacy of bifurcation here! We cannot accept the argument either that we must be *determined* by cultural bias or that we are *entirely free* of it. We can be *influenced* (even strongly) by cultural factors without those factors *determining* our every choice or decision. Cultural bias, together with the other subjective conditions we have mentioned throughout this book, does play a part in our ethical judgment. There is no getting around that fact. But the issue of cultural influence is not a matter of either/or, it is a matter of more or less. The critical question is whether we can free ourselves from those factors (by becoming aware of them, as we have proposed) *to a degree* and, if that is possible, it is sufficient for our purposes. This is what we meant when we suggested in the first chapter that objectivity in ethics (as is the case elsewhere) is a matter of degree. None of us is able to become completely free of personal and cultural encumbrances, but some of us are better able than others, and all of us can improve.

Our goal, then, is to free ourselves as much as possible from cultural bias, emotional commitment, blind conviction, and narrow vision. We can do this by becoming aware of these factors as they influence our thinking, by becoming better informed on important issues, and by trying to think more critically in order to enable ourselves to consider ethical reasons fairly and with an open mind. This is a process that must be ongoing and in ethics, where we care so deeply about the issues involved, it is particularly difficult.

Ask yourself whether this is a real possibility or merely a form of self-delusion. The key issue is whether you think the strength of arguments is merely a function of reasons that are *irreducibly* culture-bound or whether there are reasons that appeal across cultural boundaries. At this point you are in a better position to know where you stand than you were at the start of the book. You will be in an even better position to decide after you have attempted to work through some specific cases in an effort to apply the procedures we have devised in this book.

Before you proceed, however, try the following:

EXERCISE

It is extremely beneficial to the process of weighing reasons and justifying ethical claims to get at least one other point of view. Accordingly, we recommend that you make the strongest case you can for an ethical claim—any claim. Scrutinize that claim yourself, weighing reasons and strengthening the argument on your own. Now, submit the argument to one or two of your classmates and ask them to criticize your argument. (WARNING: It is important not to *personalize* criticism. Remember that criticism of an argument is directed toward the argument itself and not the person putting forth the argument. Many of us find this process threatening until we have learned that we all benefit from it, so you might want to start with an ethical claim you do not feel strongly about!)

After the group discussion, return to the argument and strengthen it even further. You will be astonished at how much better your argument is after subjecting it to this procedure than it was when you simply spun it out of your head. Don't forget to heed the warning, however!

CHAPTER FIVE

ETHICAL ARGUMENT
IN ACTION

1. THE ENVIRONMENT

Like Mom and apple pie, the environment is something everyone loves—right? Perhaps so, but not environmentalism or those environmentalists who have alienated some people in their active concern for protecting the environment. Indeed, the battles between environmentalists and anti-environmentalists have been rather heated at times, and like so many battles in ethics there is at times more heat than light. Perhaps we can provide some light by discussing at length a letter that appeared in a daily paper in Marshall, Minnesota several days before Earth Day, 1990, and then moving on to consideration of a typical case study involving some of the key issues in the controversy. We begin with the letter because it raises some interesting issues and because it will offer us an opportunity to show how to use the techniques developed in this book in a concrete example of ethical reasoning.

The letter reads as follows:

There is no question that concerns about the environment have cost Americans tens of billions of dollars and led to a marked reduction in our nation's competitive position in world markets. Not satisfied with an array of taxes, regulations, and controls they have spawned, environmental lobbyists are gearing up for another assault on

America's producers with their Earth Day 1990 scheduled for April 22nd. Yet, a growing number of scientific authorities now feel that many of the environmental claims are unsubstantiated hokum.

I am properly concerned about pollution and other threats to the environment, nevertheless I maintain that the demands of the doomsday environmentalists would have us give up personal and national freedom to address highly-speculative [sic] theories. This would be both foolish and dangerous.

For an example of environmental extremism, Earth Day 1990 Director Sen. Timothy Worth of Colorado has stated: "We've got to ride the global warming issue. . . . Even if the theory is wrong, we will be doing the right thing in terms of economic and environmental policy."

Professor Richard Lindzen of Massachusetts Institute of Technology and Jerome Namais of the Scripps Institute of Oceanography their [sic] claim that forecasts about global warming "are so inaccurate and fraught with uncertainty as to be totally useless to policy-makers [sic]."

While environmentalists call for national and international controls to combat the frightening scenarios they repeatedly paint, I claim that many supposed threats, such as those involving ozone depletion, have never been based on credible evidence. University Professor Peter Beckmann has concluded that it is ludicrous to attempt to draw any firm conclusions from the skimpy data assembled to date.

The propaganda is so intense that President Bush has succumbed. When he proclaimed April 22 to be Earth Day 1990, the president suggested "the formation of an international alliance that responds to global environmental concerns." That indicates a willingness to transfer sovereignty that is more frightening than any environmentalist's wild claim.

Yours truly,
etc.

The letter is filled with invective and loose language. Some of the terms (notably "spawned," "assault," "hokum," "doomsday," "foolish," "dangerous," and "frightening") comprise an appeal to emotion, since they slant the argument away from environmentalism without providing rational support for that slant.

There are several vague key terms. What does the author mean, for example, by "personal and national freedom"? Are these economic freedoms, as suggested in the reference to the "reduction of the nation's competitive position in world markets," or is the author referring to loss of "sovereignty"? Are these types of freedom related? If so, how?

There appear to be two conclusions connected, presumably, by the relationship (whatever it might be) between these two types of freedom. One conclusion is that we will lose our "personal and national freedom" if we listen to the "doomsday environmentalists"; the other, that President Bush's proclamation indicates a "frightening . . . transfer [of] sovereignty." Let us suppose the conclusions are somehow related. The argument would then be as follows:

(R1) Scientific evidence about pollution and "other threats to the environment" does not warrant measures leading to environmental protection.

(R2) Such protection, being unwarranted, would also lead to loss of personal freedoms, transfer of sovereignty, and a reduction of our nation's competitive position in world markets.

(C) Therefore [implied] we should not listen to doomsday environmentalists. Or: Action to protect the environment is not warranted at present, based on the skimpy evidence.

What can be said about this argument as we have stated it here? In the first place, we must assure ourselves we have represented the argument fairly. Assuming that this is so, let us proceed.

To begin with, there is little evidence that this author has attempted to adopt the ethical perspective. He is clearly not neutral on this issue and seems to be little concerned about the long run except as it might affect "loss of personal freedom." On a critical level, the argument assumes throughout that loss of "personal and national freedoms" is somehow related to a "marked reduction in our nation's competitive position in world markets." This needs to be argued, since (as we have noted above) there is some vague language here and the connection between these two items is not self-evident.

Another assumption, which we can readily grant since it accords with our first principle, is that we do not want to lose these "freedoms." A third and more important assumption (which we must question) is that this loss results directly from steps taken to protect the environment. This assumption smacks of bifurcation in that it presupposes that *either* we protect the environment, *or* we protect our personal freedoms and our position in world markets . . . *but not both*.

In the first reason stated above, we note that reference to "scientific evidence" smacks of illicit appeal to authority, since we are not told in the letter anything about the people appealed to—except that they are university professors—or whether we should lend their testimony any credence whatever. Further, these authorities have spoken only about ozone depletion, and that is not exhaustive of the class of actions we might collect in the phrase "pollution and other threats to the environment."

In addition, Senator Worth might insist that even if the increased costs cannot be avoided they must be incurred because, on balance, the consequences of failure to take steps to protect the environment may, in the long run, be even more costly, both financially and otherwise. Senator Worth seems to suggest in the quote given in the third paragraph of this letter that even if the danger to the environment is exaggerated, steps to protect it should be taken anyway, since it would be prudent to err on the side of caution in this case. The letter does not address this suggestion, so we shall take it no further; but it is a point worth noting, especially since it reflects one of the dimensions of the ethical perspective that the letter's author seems to ignore.

On balance, the argument is rather weak, and the conclusion is not warranted by the reasons given. The central connection that must be made to keep this argument afloat is that the money spent on steps taken to protect the environment invariably result in a "loss of our nation's competitive position in world markets," that is, that we cannot maintain that position and protect the environment at the same time. This bifurcation seriously weakens the argument as it does any that would insist that environmental protection *invariably* results in loss of jobs, "quality of life," and world status. The tension between jobs and protecting the environment seems to lie at the center of many of the conflicts that have arisen recently in the controversy over the protection of the environment, and we shall return to this controversy in later case studies.

* * *

For the moment, let us take a fairly simple case involving some rather straightforward environmental issues to see how our principles and procedures are applied in assembling an argument rather than dismantling it.

Scott and Sharon want to buy a car, but they can't agree which one to buy. Scott wants a Mazda MX-6 because it's a "sporty" car with good pickup and speed, and he has seen one in the showroom in candy-apple red and he is smitten.

Sharon, on the other hand, wants a Honda Civic four-door, and she has seen one at the dealer's in silver with a sporty little "bra" on the front end. The car of her choice is cheaper than Scott's, but they have agreed they can afford either car and they also agree that they could "live with" either car's appearance even though they have definite preferences. After considerable discussion, they agree to write down the reasons why they want the car of their choice and to take it from there.

Scott's reasons are as follows:

(1) Safety
(2) Environmental concerns, including economy (E.P.A. 22/28)
(3) Performance (speed and handling)
(4) Looks
(5) Cost

Sharon's reasons are as follows:

(1) Safety
(2) Environmental concerns, including economy (E.P.A. 34/38)
(3) Performance (handling, adequate speed)
(4) Looks
(5) Cost

Since they have agreed that points #4 and #5 have been covered in prior discussions, they consider them a stand-off. The argument works either way, they figure.

Eventually, they agree that point #3 is also a stand-off, because Scott has to admit that the Honda has adequate speed and handles well. However, he insists that the Mazda's added speed be considered a reinforcement of point #1, because it will allow the car to accelerate more quickly when passing and therefore avoid possible head-on collisions. Sharon counters that lower speeds are safer and whatever extra measure of safety is gained by the Mazda's additional power is lost because of the temptation to drive faster.

Next, Scott introduces insurance company data that show that larger cars are safer in accidents; the driver and passengers suffer fewer serious injuries than they would in a subcompact of the Honda variety. Sharon counters with data of her own that show that subcompacts are involved in fewer accidents. In the end they concede this is another stand-off, because the argument seems to work both ways once again. Both sides can muster equally strong reasons.

Scott and Sharon both consider themselves environmentalists (not "doomsday environmentalists," just regular environmentalists). Accordingly, they decide to purchase the Honda, because it has much better E.P.A. figures. Their reasoning is as follows:

Environmental concerns are one of the two most important factors in determining which car we will buy.

Safety, the other factor, is a stand-off.

The increased fuel economy of the Honda is a decided environmental "plus." It will use less gas, which is a finite resource, and it will burn the fuel it uses more efficiently with less carbon dioxide emission, thereby doing less damage to the ozone layer—both key environmental considerations and concerns central to the ethical perspective.

Therefore, we should buy the Honda.

Note how factual considerations enter into what is essentially an ethical argument. The argument is a strong one and the conclusion is entailed by the premises if we read the first reason as an ethical premise that states (roughly) "we should buy the car that is preferable from an environmental standpoint, all other things being equal."

The argument is strong, however, only because Sharon and Scott agree that they should protect the environment. They both accept the precept "we should buy a car that is preferable from an environmental standpoint . . ." What if either of them challenged that precept? Could it withstand criticism? Is it a *good* reason, one that *anyone* should accept? Remember, we have said repeatedly that an argument involving strict entailment (as this one does) is only as strong as its weakest link. Let us see how strong this link is.

To test this precept, we shall use the Socratic *maieutic*, what we have called the method of "proposal and disposal." That is to say, we shall propose that the precept accepted by Sharon and Scott be accepted by everyone, and see if there are any good reasons to support this proposal. If we cannot find good reasons to reject, or dispose of, this precept, then we can suppose that it is worthy of acceptance by anyone and not just Scott and Sharon.

What reasons are there to protect the environment—which is the central claim in the precept we need to defend? As ethical principles, the three principles we advanced in Chapter Two would be excellent support for our precept here. The "environment" is the world in which all sentient creatures live—including, obviously, persons, who should be respected as persons in accordance with our first principle. We have said that respect for persons is a necessary condition for ethics, and if this is so then it would appear that persons have a right to a clean environment. Polluted air damages our health and without clean water we would die, and concern for life is clearly entailed by what we are calling "respect for persons."

There may be such things as "animal rights" in addition, though we have not brought them into our argument. The notion of animal rights is troublesome, and we need not delve into the issue to make our point. We also need not consider the question of whether or not respect for persons entails rights to untrampled wilderness, or whether *future* persons (as yet unborn) have rights, though both of these claims are probable. It is enough for our present purposes to acknowledge the basic rights all persons have to a healthy life, which necessitates a clean environment, since this principle provides a good reason to protect the environment.

If this defense of our ethical principle stands, as it apparently does, then the precept we started out to defend above, to the effect that "we should protect the environment," can withstand critical scrutiny. Therefore, if Sharon can show that an economical car will burn less fuel and thus will protect the environment (more than a larger, less economical car would), her argument is quite strong, as we supposed.

2. COMPULSORY STERILIZATION

Ernest Friedman, a physician, has a patient, Georgia Hendricks, a young black woman with sickle cell anemia. She has recently delivered a baby girl. Her attacks have been fewer and less severe in recent years. However, Dr. Friedman has recently read an article indicating that if one discounts a few unusually low-risk women, women with sickle cell disease have an almost 10 percent chance of death during pregnancy. He has suggested sterilization to Georgia, but she has persistently refused. This new evidence about mortality makes him even more sure that she should be sterilized to avoid another pregnancy. He thinks that if he put the argument to her dramatically, she could probably be convinced to be sterilized. Should he ethically do so? Why or why not?*

This is an interesting case. The key term, and one which requires clarification, is the term "dramatically." Just how dramatic does Dr. Friedman plan to be? The key issue, though, is whether in putting an argument to his patient "dramatically," Dr. Friedman denies her status as a person—that is, her right to be respected as a person.

In a most important essay, to which we have referred earlier, Onora O'Neill argues that coercion, or manipulation, of one person by another constitutes a denial of the latter's status as a person; it denies that person's autonomy, or capacity to make moral judgments. This capacity differentiates persons from things in the Kantian view and underlies the first principle we defended in Chapter Two.

The central issue, according to O'Neill, is whether or not there is genuine consent, which she defines as "consent to the deeper or more fundamental aspects of another's proposal . . . ." She goes on to argue:

> To treat others as persons we must allow them *the possibility either to consent to or to dissent from what is proposed* . . . . The morally signifi-

---

* From *Professional Ethics* by Michael D. Bayles. p. 89. © 1981 by Wadsworth, Inc. Reprinted by permission of the publisher.

cant aspect of treating others as persons may lie in making their consent or dissent *possible*. . . . For example, if we coerce or deceive others, their dissent, and so their genuine consent, is in principle ruled out.[1]

The question in our present case is whether the physician denies the patient's rights as a person by presenting his argument "dramatically." Does he present his case fully and with vivid illustrations and examples in such a way that the patient could not possibly be expected to dissent? Or does he present the information fully but in such a way that *she* makes the decision whether or not to undergo the operation? The first case would be unethical; the second would be ethical—in the view presented here.

Fairness is not involved, since presumably the physician would treat *anyone* the way he treats this particular patient. Further, in allowing Georgia Hendricks to make up her own mind the physician can be said to adopt a rule that would maximize human happiness.

Note here that if Dr. Friedman coerces Georgia Hendricks he not only denies her status as an autonomous moral agent, that is, a person, but he implicitly adopts a rule that would not increase the sum of human happiness, in Aristotle's sense of that term. Persons generally deserve respect as a *necessary* condition of ethical behavior. That is to say, such a rule would not allow that persons be coerced, or manipulated, whenever another person (presumably an "authority" or an "expert") determines that the situation warrants it. Such coercion would open the door to all manner of abuses that would undermine ethical interaction among persons and decrease the sum of human happiness overall.

In this situation our principles imply that it is unethical under any circumstances to deny a person pertinent information that is necessary to make an informed choice. That is what "respect for persons" means, minimally, and it is one of the basic rights we have as persons. If Georgia Hendricks makes an informed choice, that is, if the "dramatic" presentation by Dr. Friedman is noncoercive, then we may assume that Ms. Hendricks would not upon reflection regret the decision. (That may well be the litmus test for coercion and noncoercion: does one have regrets later on?) If Dr. Friedman coerces her into making a decision she will regret later, if she has not given her *genuine consent* to the surgery, then Dr. Friedman has done the wrong thing—regardless of the consequences. Clearly, it is imperative that we know how "dramatic" Dr. Friedman plans to be!

By way of summing up, let us use the techniques devised in previous pages of this book to put together a strong argument for the most reasonable conclusion we can reach in this case.

Coercion involves the denial of one's right to be respected as a person and is therefore wrong. (Principle #1.)

Dr. Friedman's "dramatic" presentation to Ms. Hendricks does (does not) involve coercion.

Therefore, Dr. Friedman should not (should) persuade Ms Hendricks in a "dramatic" fashion to undergo sterilization.

COMMENT: As we have said, the key to this argument is the word "dramatic" and whether Dr. Friedman's manner of persuasion allows his patient to make her own decision whether or not to undergo the operation.

3. LAWYER'S PRIVILEGE

Arthur Brown is a very busy and successful attorney. Ace Retailers has hired him to defend them in a suit by a customer. The complaint was filed twenty-seven days ago and Brown has not yet filed an answer, although he has had the case for over two weeks. When the president of Ace phones Brown, he tells him that he will not file an answer until he receives a $20,000 retainer. State law requires that an answer be filed within thirty days or parties will be considered to have admitted all allegations of fact in the complaint. The president of Ace thinks the fee high even for a trial, and the case may be settled before going to trial. But since he doesn't have time to find another attorney, he sends Brown the check by courier. Is Brown's conduct unethical? If so, why? If not, why not?*

This would appear to be a fairly straightforward case, because it does not involve ethical conflict. If we were to weigh the reasons pro and con, the "pro" reasons for Brown's action would be exclusively a matter of short-run self-interest. It is difficult to see

* From *Professional Ethics* by Michael D. Bayles. p. 58. © 1981 by Wadsworth, Inc. Used by permission of the publisher.

any good ethical reasons for what appears to be a case of extortion! The ethical perspective is nowhere in evidence. The "con" reasons take the form of violations of all three of the principles we defended in Chapter Three. This example will show how to apply these principles to a specific case.

Principle #1 (involving respect for persons) has been violated because Brown has been deceitful with the president of Ace Retailers and has violated the respect due the president, who is being coerced into paying what appears to be a rather steep fee for (what might prove to be) routine procedures.

Principle #2 (involving fairness) has been violated in that this form of extortion is grossly unfair to Brown's client, who is unable to exercise his free choice to replace Brown with another attorney. No one in the "original position" would approve of this sort of treatment of one person by another, and we suspect this would include Brown himself. That is, if Brown were himself the victim of this maltreatment he would certainly not approve. Thus, from the ethical perspective the action is suspect.

Principle #3 (involving the adoption of a rule that will maximize human happiness) has been violated because Brown cannot adopt an ethical rule to engage in this sort of practice, since it does not make anyone happy except Brown himself! Ironically, it may not even make Brown truly happy. Let us see if we can make the case for this claim.

The action on Brown's part is not in Brown's best interest, though it might be in his short-run interest. In the long run, however, Brown is liable to manipulate himself out of business. The sort of treatment Brown accords the president of Ace Retailers will likely become known and Brown will gain a reputation as a crooked lawyer. Potential clients will take their business elsewhere rather than fall victim to Brown's underhanded treatment. Whether or not Brown chooses to act ethically—and it may be difficult to do so and survive as a "busy and successful attorney"— it would be prudent for him to act in accordance with his own long-run, or "best" interest.

Let us put our findings in the form of a strong ethical argument:

> Consistent with respect for persons and fairness, one should adopt a rule that will maximize human happiness.

Brown cannot adopt such a rule in this case, since his treatment
of his client is both disrespectful—involving as it does
manipulation—and unfair.

Therefore, Brown should not treat his client in the manner
described.

* * *

An interesting question arises in connection with the application of
the first principle to this case. Does the principle of respect for
persons mean that persons are entitled to information they do not
request? In this case, the president of Ace Retailers did not ask
when Brown intended to file his brief—one suspects he did not
consider the question necessary. That oversight cost him dearly,
and we can say that the withholding of the information resulted in
his being coerced into paying an exorbitant fee. But what if the
withholding of information from someone works to that person's
advantage? What about the use of placebos in medicine?

Suppose, for example, that a placebo could effectively cure a
chronically ill patient and in the process save that patient a great
deal of money? Clearly, the success of placebos necessitates
secrecy—if the patients know they are taking sugar pills, the pills
are not likely to work! Is it ethically right to withhold information
in cases such as these when secrecy is essential to the success of the
treatment?

This is a very complicated case, but I do not see how we could
justify this sort of thing—even if it works—because it violates our
first principle. That is, whether or not the placebo works (and at
times they do not), the patient has been denied the right to make
an informed choice and is therefore a victim of coercion.

Consider the difficulty of finding an acceptable rule to cover this
case, a rule that will maximize the happiness of all persons. The
placebo experiment might work in the majority of cases, though
this is a moot point, but the rule would advocate the use of coercion as a means to a possible cure, making it a difficult rule to
adopt, from an ethical perspective.

However, there is an added dimension in this case that is of
central importance. A tacit understanding exists between a patient
and a physician that may well provide a basis for ethical justification in the case of the use of placebos. The patient, it might be said,

goes to the physician to be cured and presumably trusts the physician to do whatever is necessary to bring about that cure. If this "whatever is necessary" includes the use of deception, it could be argued that the patient *chooses* to be deceived. In this view, the patient waives his or her rights to complete honesty and total information if the remedy will work. This seems a bit bizarre, but we all do this every time we take a prescribed drug not knowing what chemicals the drug contains or what its effects might be; and even the most vociferous defender of free choice and autonomy might well agree that the doctor/patient relationship provides an exceptional case.

If we choose this line of reasoning, we could formulate and adopt a rule that patients may choose to suspend their right to informed choice in the interest of their own health. But it must remain the patient's choice and must not be forced upon him or her by the physician or else the patient's rights have been denied.

The argument would look like this:

Coercion, as a rule, is ethically wrong.

Coercion is involved when physicians deny their patients the right to make decisions involving their own health.

Coercion is not involved, on the other hand, if patients waive their right to know every aspect of their treatment, if such knowledge would interfere with the success of the treatment.

Medical treatment involving the use of placebos can only succeed if the patients are ignorant that they are receiving placebos.

Thus, the use of placebos is not coercive, and it does not violate any other ethical rules.

Therefore, the use of placebos is ethically permissible.

4. WHISTLEBLOWING

Marlene and Steve live in Clotilda, California, a city of 80,000. Steve works at EMC, the local chemical plant, as a design engineer at a very good salary. They have a three-month-old baby who has just been diagnosed as having a rare liver cancer that may be untreatable. The young couple, devastated by the news, begin to question local agencies in an attempt to discover the possible causes of the baby's malady. They discover some startling facts: an unusually large number of cases of liver cancer has been reported in the past seven years in Clotilda, especially among very young children and infants, who do not usually contract this particular form of cancer. In addition, young women in the area have experienced three times the normal number of miscarriages in the past six years, and the area has had three and one half times the usual number of birth defects in the past six or seven years.

Steve takes some water samples to the local pollution control agent, who has them tested. The results show that the water contains measurable quantities of dioxin, a known carcinogen, and Steve begins to suspect that the origin of this contamination is chemical waste that he knows EMC has been burying for the past ten or eleven years in a deserted landfill near the chemical plant. He has reason to believe that leakage from the chemical waste is finding its way into the city's water supply. Subsequent investigation confirms this suspicion.

Steve approaches his supervisor at EMC to bring the problem to the attention of company officials in order to see what, if anything, can be done to clean up the dump site and eliminate the problem at its source. Upon pressing his inquiry to his increasingly uneasy supervisor, Steve realizes that the company has been aware of the problem for some time and has simply "covered it up." Steve's supervisor strongly urges him to "keep his mouth shut" and "do his job—or he won't have any job to do!"

Steve returns home and he discusses their options with Marlene. Above all else, they both want to do the right thing. This is the list of options they come up with:

(1) Follow his supervisor's advice.
(2) Quit the job and take another elsewhere.
(3) "Blow the whistle" on the company to force it to clean up the water and the landfill, even though this will result in Steve's losing his job—along with others who will probably be laid off when company profits dip as a result of the clean up.
(4) Quit the job and take EMC to court to try to close the plant.
What should they do?

Steve and Marlene decide on the third option. Their reasoning is as follows: Alternative #1 would be prudent, but not ethical. On a personal level, additionally, they would find it difficult to go on as if nothing had happened knowing what they do. Alternative #2 would solve *their* problem but not *the* problem. Many of their friends in Clotilda would remain behind, drinking contaminated water. Alternative #4 is impractical because Steve cannot afford the high costs of hiring a lawyer and the expenses of a protracted court battle against a wealthy chemical company.

Alternative #3 is the only acceptable alternative from the ethical perspective. Even though it will cost Steve his job, along with a number of his coworkers at EMC, Steve and Marlene reason that the company will be forced by local and federal officials, together with bad publicity, into cleaning up the landfill and stopping the leakage into the water supply. In addition, the residents of Clotilda will be made aware of a situation about which they are currently ignorant. They see the conflict as one between jobs, on the one hand, and the health of the city, on the other hand.

From the ethical perspective, Steve is concerned about the rights of others to a clean and healthful environment, and he adopts a rule that will maximize the happiness of the majority of persons affected by that rule.

At this point, Steve's argument would look something like this:

The current situation involving the discharge of toxic chemicals is intolerable from an ethical perspective.
The only effective option appears to be to blow the whistle.
I have adequate documentation and I have good reason to believe that the situation will be remedied.
Therefore, I should blow the whistle.

The situation is a bit simple as we have described it, of course. The reader is probably wondering about Steve's obligations to his family. As we presented the case, Steve and Marlene made the decision together, and we assume they would share a sense of obligation to the wider community and are prepared to face the harsh realities of finding a new job and paying what will probably be very large medical bills for their child. But we have ignored their obligations to their child. What about these obligations?

The new dimension doesn't change the ethical priorities in this case. Steve still has an obligation to blow the whistle, and he will surely lose his job as a result. The practical difficulties, though very real and pressing, are ethically irrelevant. As Steve and Marlene weigh the pros and cons of this situation, their love for their child and their awareness of the practical difficulties will surely enter in. But there do not appear to be any good, compelling reasons to agree with the objection that Steve and Marlene are ignoring their obligations to their child, or that this obligation overrides their obligation to the many who will contract cancer if they continue to drink contaminated water. From an ethical perspective, obligations are to *persons* and do not vary depending on who the person happens to be or what the relationship of that person is to the ethical agent. Steve and Marlene will surely *feel* a stronger obligation to their child than to 79,997 nonrelations in Clotilda. But this does not make the obligation more compelling from an ethical perspective, which requires neutrality.

But, surely it will be argued, we have ignored the rights of the baby. Perhaps the baby's rights must be considered equally with those of all other persons, but they must be considered, somehow! We have simply ignored them to this point. Surely, the baby has the right to medical treatment, even if this treatment is likely not to help. We have stated in Chapter Two that respect for persons is a necessary condition to ethical action. Can't we be charged with inconsistency or even downright contradiction? (Steve and Marlene are doing the right thing to blow the whistle even though in doing so they fail to treat their own child as a person which we have stated is a necessary condition to ethical action. This would appear to be a contradiction, indeed.) Let us reflect.

The only way we could agree that the baby's rights have been ignored is if Steve and Marlene deny the baby medical treatment, to which (admittedly) all persons have a right if that treatment has even a slight chance of saving the person's life. But even if we agree that medical treatment cannot be denied the baby without ignoring the baby's rights, it is not clear in this case that medical treatment *cannot* be supplied by Steve and Marlene unless Steve keeps *this particular job*. That is, the baby's rights are not being ignored *because* Steve blows the whistle and loses his job. (Beware the bifurcation: *either* Steve keeps this job *or* he denies his baby's right to medical attention. This is simplistic.) The baby's rights would be ignored only if this series of events necessarily involved the denial of medical treatment for the baby, which they do not. There is no contradiction.

At this point, if Steve and Marlene were to put the argument together, it might look like this:

> The current situation involving the discharge of toxic chemicals is intolerable from an ethical perspective.
> Blowing the whistle appears to be the only effective remedy.
> I have obligations to the residents of Clotilda, but I also have obligations to my family.
> My obligations to my family require that I continue to make a living and try to find medical treatment for my child. Presumably, I can do both in another town.
> My obligations to the residents of Clotilda require that I blow the whistle, thereby informing them of the danger involved in drinking the city water, and, presumably, forcing the chemical company to remedy the situation.
> Therefore, I should blow the whistle.

We could, of course, persist in modifying the example by insisting that there is absolutely no way Steve and Marlene could provide medical treatment for their child unless Steve keeps his present job—which is highly unlikely. But if this were the case, then we would have to conclude that Steve and Marlene cannot do the right thing in this case, because in doing one right thing (getting medical treatment for the baby or making it known that the city's water is contaminated) they must do a wrong thing (deny the baby's rights to medical treatment or deny the rights of the citizens of Clotilda to uncontaminated drinking water). This is an essentially *tragic* situation, that is, a situation in which there appears to be no right thing to do—though R. M. Hare would disagree, as we saw in Chapter Two.

Fortunately, these situations are as rare as they are painful for those involved.

As if things weren't bad enough, the problem described here would be even more complicated, from an ethical perspective, if the chemicals did not pose a health hazard to the people of Clotilda, or if they only posed a *potential* health hazard. (Notice how these contingencies would weaken the various premises in Steve and Marlene's argument as we stated it above.) It would also be more complicated if the hazard were posed to nonhumans.

Take the case of "Butterflies vs Industry," described by Ken Peterson (*San Jose Mercury*, October 25, 1979) as an example:

A large semiconductor company called Synertex proposed opening a $40 million research and manufacturing plant in Santa Cruz, California, across the street from Natural Bridges State Park. The plant would employ 350–400 workers. The problem arose when it was discovered that the plant would occasionally (about 20% of the time) release small amounts of hydrocarbons, sulfur and nitrogen oxides into the air upwind from the park where approximately 95,000 monarch butterflies congregate each year in their annual migrations. It was not known whether or not the fumes from the plant would harm the butterflies. From an ethical perspective, should the plant be allowed to be built at that site? Possibly a compromise might be worked out here (e.g., further testing of the effects of the fumes on the butterflies, relocation of the plant downwind etc.). But if it is not possible to find a middle ground then the ethical conflict is in the form of a dilemma, one side of which concerns the jobs of 350–400 people and the other side of which concerns the damage to the butterflies and possibly to the ecosystem of which they are a part.

Some would argue that "animal rights" are at issue here, but, as mentioned above, we have not introduced this troublesome notion because it is not clear what it means, strictly speaking. Besides, it could be argued that humans have an obligation to protect the environment and its nonhuman inhabitants on the grounds that we should adopt rules that maximize human happiness— including, in this case, future generations. Further, it might be argued that respect for ourselves as persons involves humane treatment of helpless animals and respect for the environment.

Furthermore, even though we might agree that a person has a right to "make a living," or at any rate to the means necessary for survival, it is not clear that one could argue that a person has a right to a *particular* job.

What do *you* think?

CHAPTER SIX

CASES FOR DISCUSSION AND ANALYSIS

This chapter includes a number of case studies for purposes of analysis and discussion. The studies will be arranged in groups with some suggestions provided to help you with the first case in each group. You should not feel bound by the suggestions, but they might be helpful in getting you started.

Try to use the procedure outlined in the text when possible to help you prepare ethical arguments. Weigh reasons using the Socratic *maieutic* and try to focus your attention on the central question: what *should* a person (any person) do in this situation? Ignore the question of what a person might do (in fact). You might not agree that ethics should ignore practical considerations, but it will be helpful in working through the ethical issues if you keep the practical questions in abeyance at first. Ethical issues involving conflicts are extremely difficult to sort out and resolve. But if we are trying to decide what we would do at the same time we are trying to decide what we should do, the matter becomes even more complicated. Keep in focus the related questions: what *principles* are involved here? What is the *right* thing to do?

1. GENERAL ISSUES

G1. You are a member of a school board in a fairly large city in Ohio. One of the tenth-grade teachers who has taught at your school for six years and who has a reputation as a gifted teacher has just "come out of the closet" and announced that he is gay. The members of the school board want him fired. What should you do?

SUGGESTIONS: Focus on the key issue: What does respect for the teacher as a person involve in this case? Weigh respect for the teacher against the rights of the students and the possible harm that could come from confrontation with this teacher. Try to be realistic and consider carefully whether or not it is reasonable to expect harm to come to the students in this situation. Try to be clear what "harm" could mean in this context. Think, also, of the possible harm that could come to the teacher from being fired from this job.

G2. Jane has just been told by her doctor that she has contracted chlamydia from one or more of the young men she has had sexual contact with recently. Her concern is whether or not to tell her latest date, Dave—toward whom she has very strong feelings. She agrees, on her doctor's advice, to begin taking a prescription drug that should have an effect on the disease in a week or so, but she decides not to tell Dave for fear that she will lose him. In the meantime she decides to let things take their natural course. If they should sleep together—and she hopes they will—she's convinced herself "it's not like it's AIDS or something; if he gets it, he can get treated the same way I did." Did Jane do the right thing? If so, why? If not, why not?

G3. Sid Ramey is a member of a school board in a small town in Kansas. He has two children who are in the third and fourth grades and he is faced with a problem.

A theatre company from Kansas State University has been touring the rural areas staging plays for local schools for a very nominal fee. One of the plays they routinely perform is *Lysistrata*, a Greek play that is reputed to be rather bawdy (even in the "watered down" version the company has selected). The sentiment on the board is fairly strong to deny the group's request to perform at their school. They have heard from people in towns where the play has been performed that it is "pornographic" and "sexist." What should Sid do (1) as a parent, and (2) as a member of the school board?

G4. Nancy Quincey is on the city council of a small town in West Texas. The town has recently fallen on hard times and unemployment is rather high. Representatives from Texas Power and Light have approached the city council and proposed that they build and operate a nuclear reactor in the town. The plant will employ sixty-five people during construction and forty on a regular basis during operation. Nancy has heard that such plants can be dangerous and recalls the accident at Chernobyl. What should she do?

G5. On a hot August night in the Bronx, Paul Gilman and his friend Jesus Marcos were returning from a pool hall where they had spent the last four and a half hours playing pool and drinking beer. They decided to stop at a convenience store to pick up some more beer. Neither man remembered much that happened after that, but at Gilman's trial two months later it was determined that he had an argument with the sales girl over the price of the beer, pulled a gun and shot her between the eyes. As he ran from the store, he shot two customers who were on their way in; one died instantly and the other was permanently injured.

Eileen Thomas is sitting on the jury listening to the testimony and to the prosecutor, who insists upon the death penalty for Gilman. How should she vote?

G6. Sarah Douglas sits on the U.S. Commission on World Hunger. The commission is debating whether to increase U.S. aid to third-world countries to assist in relieving the problems of starvation in those countries. Amid the deluge of information about the numbers of starving people in undeveloped countries, Sarah is confronted by the following disagreement:

One member of the Commission argues that U.S. aid must be increased if America is to resume its place as a humanitarian leader in the world. He argues that it is a matter of self-interest on the part of the U.S. to "anticipate a problem rather than wait for it to become a crisis."

Others argue that much of the money spent to alleviate world hunger is wasted because it never gets to the starving people; furthermore, even if it does reach those people, it simply exacerbates the real problem, which is population control. The argument insists that the money should be spent on birth control clinics and the education of ignorant populations rather than getting caught "on the treadmill of feeding the world's hungry masses." Money spent on feeding these people is "misguided humanitarianism," it is argued. Next to the possibility of a starvation crisis "the population explosion is considerably more threatening and terrifying to the rest of the civilized world."

How should Sarah vote on the issue of whether or not to increase U.S. aid to help reduce world hunger?

G7. Jane Harney picks up some "pin money" by raising rabbits and selling them to local pet stores. Lately she has a new client: a local laboratory has ordered a dozen, though Jane has heard that the lab will use the rabbits for experiments in the development of perfumes. As new chemicals are introduced, they are sprayed into the rabbits' eyes to determine their safety for human use. On occasion, the rabbits are blinded.

Jane is not dependent upon the income from the sales of the rabbits, but the laboratory has offered to buy twelve a week on a regular basis if she can keep up with the demand. The money would go a long way to paying off some bills and letting her put some away "for a rainy day." What should Jane do?

2. SPORTS

S1. At the age of 17 William "Willie" Smith was caught dealing drugs. While he was awaiting trial he enrolled at a local Junior College and later transferred to a small four-year college in Iowa to study and to play football, which he did very well. In the interim he was tried and found guilty of the drug charge, but he was given a delayed sentence to allow him to complete his college degree. After the completion of his degree he was to serve a nine-year prison sentence.

Willie's understanding was that his case would be reviewed at the end of his college career and that he would almost certainly be placed on probation if he "kept his nose clean," which he did. He continued work on his degree, and he played football so well he was drafted by an N.F.L. team in the ninth round. When it was announced that he had been drafted, a reporter in his home town ran a story about his brush with the law. In the ensuing confusion the judge who had tried Willie's case three years previously held a press conference and, noting that athletes should not be given special treatment, repeated her ruling that Willie was to serve nine years in prison as soon as he completed his college degree. She insisted that she never intended to review the case. The N.F.L. team that had drafted Willie announced soon thereafter that it was no longer interested in Willie Smith.

Did the judge do the right thing?

SUGGESTION: Remember that what is legal is not necessarily the same thing as what is ethically right. Courts—and judges—interpret the law; they are not necessarily concerned with what is right. Review our discussion in Chapter Two about justice as fairness. Is the judge's decision in this case "fair"? If we grant that punishment is necessary, is prison the only, or the best, form of punishment?

S2. Scott Boyer is a tennis coach at a small school near St. Cloud, Minnesota. He has a good boys' team; they have a chance this year to win their Region and go to the State Tournament. He knows that several other coaches in his region "stack" their lineups to place stronger players against weaker ones so that even though some matches are lost, the team totals will favor their teams. He has never done this, since the rules of his sport clearly state that teams are to play "in the rank order of ability," but he knows that if he follows this rule (while others do not) his team will almost certainly not win the Regional Tournament. What should he do?

S3. Pete Dimmer has been recruited to play football at Booster University. He is 6'3" tall, weighs 200 pounds, and was an outstanding high school linebacker. At Booster, however, he is not as quick or as strong as his teammates and may not get to play the sport he loves. If he does not make the team he will lose his scholarship, and since he cannot afford to go to college otherwise, he will have to drop out.

Most of Pete's teammates use steroids, and his coach has told him repeatedly that he must "bulk up," which he knows is an invitation to use steroids himself. (At the very least, none of the coaches has told him *not* to use steroids, and he can see for himself what an advantage they give to the other players.) What should Pete do?

S4. Patsy Wells coaches a women's basketball team in a small college in the Pacific Northwest. She has her eye on an outstanding college prospect, Julie, who is 6′2″ tall and can run circles around every player in her Conference. Julie will probably never make it to the State Tournament because she plays for a weak team; as a result few coaches know about Julie's ability on the basketball court. The problem is that Julie has done poorly in her schoolwork in high school and will not be admitted to college unless she goes to a local Community College for a couple of years and gets her grades up. If she does this, however, she will almost certainly play basketball, and other coaches will discover what a fine player she is. As a result, she will be heavily recruited and Patsy, whose budget is stretched to its limits, will almost certainly lose her to another school with a healthier budget. In addition, to win the Conference, Patsy needs a power forward this year and doesn't want to wait two years. Julie really wants to play for Patsy and doesn't want to wait two years, either.

As it happens, Patsy has a friend in the Admissions Department who is willing to alter Julie's records to make it appear that she has done acceptable work to this point. What should Patsy do?

S5. Monica Velez coaches gymnastics at the local high school in Peavey, New Mexico. She has a fairly good team, but she hasn't yet figured out how to get the best performance out of her gymnasts. She is convinced that she has three girls who are good enough to make the State Tournament and possibly even get scholarship offers to college—if only they would realize their full potential.

Monica reads about the use of liquid B vitamins that can be administered just under the tongue and go to work almost immediately to provide extra strength and energy. A great many athletes, especially weight lifters, use the vitamins just before competition. Even though their use is still considered experimental, their success has been remarkable. The vitamins can be purchased at the local drug store, and Monica decides to give them a try.

At the next gymnastics meet, Monica gives her team the vitamins and they perform beyond her wildest expectations, winning the meet and qualifying two of her gymnasts for the State Tournament. For some reason the girls are not the least bit curious about the drops Monica administers to them, so she decides not to say what they are.

Monica has read that because the vitamins are administered to an extremely sensitive area, they have been known to cause cancer in some persons who use them. The label on the bottle of vitamins warns against "continued use" and "abuse" of the liquid, but Monica reasons that if her team uses the vitamins only before team competition, but not in practice, and if she has them stop at the end of the season, this will not constitute "continued use" or "abuse." In addition, her team will be able to perform better than ever and possibly even win the State Tournament. What should Monica do?

S6. John Lenz coaches basketball at Wilamet College. His teams have not done very well lately and his job is on the line. He is confident that this year will be a good one, however, because he has had an excellent year recruiting. He has watched several captain's practices involving three of this year's new players and one, Jeff Green, is outstanding. Jeff transferred to Wilamet from a junior college where he was a Junior College All-American.

More than anything else, Jeff wants his college degree. He figures that he is not good enough to play professional basketball, and he looks forward to teaching and coaching young players. Jeff is John's advisee.

During Fall preregistration for Winter term, Jeff brings John a proposed course schedule that includes three difficult courses, one of which is a science course that involves a lab two afternoons a week—during basketball practice. John recommends a lighter schedule, and one without science labs that conflict with practice. The problem is that the courses Jeff chose are required for his major, and they will not be offered again for another two years.

Jeff needs to take the courses he has proposed in order to graduate on time, and he is willing to take the science course even though he will miss practice twice a week. He suggests that he can practice on his own to make up for the missed practice sessions. John knows that missing two days of practice each week will reduce Jeff's effectiveness and make it very difficult for him to work well with the other players. Shooting baskets on his own in the gym twice a week is no substitute for practice with the team. It is even possible that Jeff will have difficulty with one or two of the courses and will not be eligible next year. John's dreams of an outstanding season seem to be going up in smoke. What should he do?

S7. An extremely gifted young professional basketball player by the name of Jason Mitchel has discovered that he has contracted the HIV virus and will be forced to retire from the game. In a very candid interview with a major sports magazine, he reveals that he has had sex with over two thousand women during his years on the pro tour—many of them after he may have contracted the virus. He is generally regarded in the press and by the public as a "hero" for coming forward and facing the issue honestly and without flinching. In addition, Mitchel had indicated that he would begin to speak out to young people about the dangers of AIDS and contribute a considerable amount of his own money to AIDS research.

In a later issue of the same sports magazine, one of the senior editors, Edith Wylder, argued that Mitchel should not be regarded as a hero for his involvement in what many people would consider irresponsible sexual behavior. Most people tended to ignore the fact that Mitchel may have infected any number of women with the HIV virus. Wylder argued that Mitchel's status as a hero or a villain will be determined by his actions in the future rather than his past behavior. She added that a woman would have been roundly criticized if it were revealed that she had slept with two thousand men. She argued that society was applying a double standard in this case, an argument substantiated by the revelation in the press that such behavior is quite common among professional athletes—one of whom boasted that he had slept with twenty thousand women in his professional career!

What do *you* think?

3. MEDICINE

M1. Sally Curtis is a night nurse at the emergency room at the local hospital. Late one night when the emergency room is practically deserted, a policeman brings in a young man with a critical stab wound. The policeman has brought the man to this hospital because it is closest and, in his opinion, the young man could not have survived a trip to another hospital. The problem is that the young man has no identification, and there can be no way to know whether he has hospital insurance. From the look of him he has none. Sally has already been admonished several times for admitting patients without proper identification and proof of insurance. One more time and she is liable to lose her job. What should she do?

SUGGESTIONS: Try to keep the issue of short-run self-interest separate from the ethical problem here. Note, for example, how the issue changes if Sally is the sole support for her husband and three children or if she is single. Consider Sally's obligations to the hospital as well as her obligations to herself and to the young man. If Sally refuses the young man treatment and he later dies, is she an accessory to murder—even though she didn't raise a hand against him? Can she *justify* her role in the young man's death by saying she did nothing to harm him—or is this *rationalization*? Put together an argument that could withstand criticism by a disinterested third person.

M2. Thomas and Emily have been married for forty-seven years. Emily has developed Alzheimer's Disease, and her condition has deteriorated to the point where she doesn't recognize her husband when he visits her hospital room. While she is not in extreme pain, her husband finds it difficult to visit and see the way she is treated by the hospital staff and note the total lack of awareness she seems to have of her surroundings. It will not get any better, and Thomas recalls conversations he had with Emily in the early stages of her disease when they both agreed what they would do when "the time came." Recalling those conversations, and in the midst of a cloud of doubt and anguish, Thomas walks into Emily's hospital room, puts a .22 caliber pistol to her temple and pulls the trigger.

Did he do the right thing?

M3. Dr. Herold Goldstein specializes in kidney diseases. He has three patients in critical condition, all of whom are on dialysis machines waiting for a kidney donor. One of the patients is a seven-year-old boy. Another is a thirty-five-year old mother of three children whose husband has recently filed for divorce. The third is a former all-pro cornerback who now, at the age of forty-two, coaches football at the local high school. A donor is found who can provide a kidney for one of the patients, but the likelihood is that another will not be found in time to help the other two patients. Which of the three patients should Dr. Goldstein select for the donor kidney, and why?

M4. Elaine Fedder, a sixteen-year-old pregnant woman who wants an abortion, visits the local Planned Parenthood organization. She requests that they not notify her parents that she has been there. Later that day, nurse Clyde Davis phones Elaine at home. When Elaine's mother answers, he does not leave his name or that of the Planned Parenthood organization, but he does leave his phone number, asking Elaine's mother to have Elaine phone him when she returns. Elaine's mother immediately phones the number and discovers that it is the Planned Parenthood organization. She confronts Elaine and forces her to have the baby and marry the baby's father, a seventeen-year-old high school student. Was nurse Davis unethical in leaving his phone number? Why or why not? Do parents have an ethical right to be informed of medical treatment for their children? If so, at what age does that right cease—or doesn't it?

M5. Asher Bausch and his wife are both Ashkenazic Jews. They went to the local genetics unit to be tested for the chances of having a child with Tay Sachs disease. This recessive genetic disorder is untreatable and produces blindness, motor paralysis, and other symptoms leading to death, usually before the age of three. The tests showed that Asher was a carrier, but that his wife was not. While he and his wife were not at risk of having a child with the birth defect, Asher's brothers had a 50 percent chance of being carriers, and if either of them married an Ashkenazic Jew, the chances were 1 in 30 that the wife would be a carrier and so the odds were 1 in 60 that they would have an affected infant. Dr. Cloe Dunlop asked Asher to send his brothers a letter that the genetics unit had prepared suggesting that they be tested for the carrier status. Asher became upset and refused. He felt ashamed and could not bring himself to tell his brothers. Would it be ethical for Dr. Dunlop to write the brothers and recommend to them that they have genetic screening? Why or why not?

M6. A psychiatrist, Gerri Hudson, is treating Irwin Johnson, who was referred to her as being near a nervous breakdown. After a few sessions, Irwin confesses to having murdered a child six months before. Gerri does not think Irwin will murder again and thinks that she can assist him, whether or not he turns himself in to the police—as he is thinking of doing. What should Gerri do? Why?

4. LAW

L1. Edgar Farr is representing his client who has been convicted on a criminal charge. They are now before the judge for sentencing. The judge asks the clerk if Farr's client has a previous criminal record, and the clerk says he has not. However, Edgar knows that his client does have a record. While he is trying to decide what to do the judge says, "As this is your first offence, I shall give you a suspended sentence." What should Farr do? Why?

SUGGESTIONS: Think about whether telling an untruth when asked a direct question is a lie in the same sense that silence in a case such as this might be. Are both unethical? Equally so? Keep Edgar's self-interest out of the issue until the end. If Edgar's silence is tantamount to a lie, would it be wrong in this case? Can Edgar simply say to himself: "The clerk made the mistake; it's not my problem"? Would this be rationalizing? Make a case for Edgar, one way or the other, that can withstand your own critical scrutiny and that of your classmates.

L2. Leslie Jacobsen is a young and talented lawyer who has been with the Public Defender's Office in Los Angles for seven years. She has recently been assigned to defend Amos Pritchard, a man accused of a series of brutal murders. This is the first time she has been assigned to such an important case with sole responsibility for the client's defense. In her conversations with Pritchard, however, it becomes clear to Leslie that the man is guilty not only of the murders mentioned in the indictment, but also of several others, and that he is likely to kill again if found not guilty and released. She tries to convince Pritchard to plead "not guilty by virtue of insanity" and seek psychiatric help. He refuses and becomes outraged at her suggestion that he might be "nuts."

Just before Pritchard's case is scheduled to come to trial, the police arrest a homeless drug addict who confesses to the murders Pritchard has been accused of. Leslie knows she can get her client off—but should she? What should she do?

L3. George Howard is an activist lawyer with political ambitions. A couple of years ago he prosecuted a suit that struck down the racial and sexual discriminatory practices of a local corporation. He is also vice president of a local environmental organization. The corporation's factory is now being forced to close due to new local regulations on pollution. The local black organization, which considers him its lawyer, wishes to join the corporation's management in attacking the local regulations on pollution so that the factory can remain open. George would represent the blacks who obtained jobs as a result of his earlier case. The suit will probably be opposed by the environmental organization to which George belongs. What should he do? Why?

L4. Attorney Kevin Stone is representing Humboldt, Inc. in a contract negotiation with the Joiner's Union. They are fairly close to an agreement on a wage increase, but both sides are intransigent. To get things moving, the union's chief negotiator, Marcia Lockhardt, phones Kevin and offers the following compromise: Humboldt will agree to release ten employees who do not belong to the union and who are not essential to the company's operations. In turn, Marcia promises that the union will accept a wage agreement closer to Humboldt's terms, and Humboldt could save more than enough to meet the union's wage demands. The contract could be settled without further delay. What should Kevin recommend? Why?

L5. Amy Pivec, a young and upcoming corporation lawyer, has been subpoenaed to appear before a Grand Jury seeking an indictment against Trilux Corporation for violations of antitrust laws and six counts of extortion and bribery in connection with an earlier case. Amy is close friends with Michael Brown, an executive in Trilux with whom Amy has spent considerable time. Michael is one of the executives named in the indictment and Amy will be asked to reveal information Michael told her in strict confidence— not as his lawyer, but as his friend. If Amy does not reveal the information she will almost certainly be found in contempt of court and may face disbarment proceedings. She knows that some of the information Michael has disclosed to her will get both Michael and Trilux into serious trouble. What should she do?

5. BUSINESS

B1. You are an engineering consultant to mining firms. Surestrike Mining hires you to do two jobs for $5,000 each. One is to evaluate a potential mine you are already familiar with; you are sure that your report will be negative. Should you accept the job?

The second job is to evaluate a productive mine. You discover that the mine has moved to an adjacent property owned by East Texas Mining Company and that Surestrike does not have the mineral rights to the coal being mined there.

You report to Surestrike that they are infringing on the mineral rights of East Texas Mining. They thank you and pay you the money they owe for your fee.

Six months later you discover that Surestrike is still mining under the property owned by East Texas Mining and that they have not notified the latter company of your findings. Your contract with Surestrike provided that you would not disclose any findings to a third party. What should you do?

SUGGESTIONS: Try to keep the legal and the ethical issues separate, and keep both separate from the practical issues! Whether or not a contract you signed is legally binding it may or may not be ethically binding. Ethics is a matter of principles and when laws conflict with ethical principles some would argue that ethics must take precedence. Martin Luther King, Jr. argued this in his "Letter From a Birmingham Jail." In any event, the issues must be kept separate. Would it make any difference in this case if you were single or a married person with several other people dependent upon your income? Along this line, suppose that you know you will be blackballed in the mining industry if word gets out that you have "snitched" on Surestrike. Is this an ethical consideration, or a purely practical consideration?

B2. Kevin Black is an aspiring young management trainee with a large chemical company in New Jersey. His supervisor calls him one day and tells him that he is to assume responsibility for the burial of waste materials that are known to contain toxic substances that cause cancer in humans. He is told to take care of the waste material in the cheapest and quickest way possible. Research leaves him with only three options: (1) bury the waste near a small town of 350 people. There is a probability of 40% that the waste material will leak into the drinking water of the town and prove dangerous to the health of the residents. This way is the most expensive. (2) Bury the waste in a rural area that is destined to become a golf course and is currently mostly farms. There are several dozen families in the area of the waste site. The waste will almost certainly seep into the ground water because of the high sand content in the soil. This way is almost as cheap as the third option. (3) Bury the waste in a swamp near a city of 7500 where the likelihood is two in ten that the waste will leak into the water supply and harm the residents. This is the cheapest way to dispose of the waste chemicals. What should Kevin do?

B3. Jill Gunderson is employed as a research technician by Goodhealth Drug Company. She ran a series of tests of Colstop on mice. She wrote in her report that many of the mice developed cataracts and lost hair when injected with the drug. She later saw the report that went to top level management of Goodhealth and which also went to the F.D.A. Several of her sentences had been deleted and the cataracts were not mentioned. She reported the omission to her superiors, who became angry and told her to go back and change her original report so there is no mention of the cataracts.

Jill earns $26,000 a year at the job and is the widowed mother of three children. Jobs of this caliber are hard to find. What should she do? Why?

B4. Your company sells only in the state of New Wyoming. State law does not prohibit marketing your cola in "giant quarts," which is an advertising phrase that describes a quart bottle. However, a survey conducted by your firm indicates that 40% of cola buyers think that the "giant quart" is larger than the standard quart.

Should you market your "giant quart"?

B5. Steven Boyd, a second-year MBA student in a top business school in the Chicago area, believes he probably will go to work right after graduation for one of seven firms that already have offered him a job. He continues, however, to arrange interviews through the school's placement office. He reasons that the experience is valuable and that he may even turn up a better job.

Two companies invite him to New York City to visit their home offices. Steven plans the visits on consecutive days. He stays a night in a hotel in New York, for which one of the firms had agreed to pay, since it scheduled his interview at an early-morning hour. But Steven charges both firms for the full cost of his round trip transportation. He tells himself that because each firm said he should send in an expense account, he is not getting anything the companies did not expect to pay. One firm did not even ask him to submit receipts. Steven interprets this to mean that the firm really intended to give him the money as a gift.

Did Steven act unethically? If so, why? If not, why not? If you were an employer, knowing what you do about Steven Boyd, would you hire him? Explain fully.

B6. Margaret Larsen is the Personnel Director for a large manufacturing firm that has recently built a plant in the heart of Chicago's South Side. The company is hiring both skilled and unskilled employees and Margaret decides, on her own, that the company should hire a large proportion of blacks since the plant is located in a predominantly black neighborhood. The proportion of blacks who apply for jobs is about 67 percent, but Margaret manages to hire 83 percent, though the percentage is slightly less in the skilled group than in the unskilled group. Her hope is that some of the unskilled workers will be promoted and the percentages will even out eventually. Should Margaret have taken it upon herself to adopt such an aggressive hiring policy? Is it a policy that her company should adopt—whether or not Margaret had decided to do so? Explain fully.

6. THE ENVIRONMENT

E1. Pete Stigma is a foreman for the International Logging Company in Sweet Home, Oregon. His company laid off seventy-four people in the last two years and closed one of its three mills. Recent legislation setting aside millions of acres of first-growth pine to save the spotted owl will result in more layoffs and perhaps the closing of another mill. Pete's job is relatively secure because he has been with the company for many years, has seniority, and will retire soon anyway. But the jobs of many of his friends are in jeopardy.

Pete's company orders him to begin logging away from the gravel roads in areas that he knows are within the habitat conservation area (HCA). Because of the remoteness of the area, however, and the rapidity with which new machinery makes it possible to clear-cut the area, he knows that the operation probably won't be spotted until it is completed. At that time, if the operation is noted, the company will pay a small fine and simply pass the cost of the fine along to the customers with a slight price increase.

Pete has always considered himself a conservationist and loves the wild area that he has grown up in. But the "preservationists" back East have made him increasingly angry, because of their persistent meddling in an area that they have never even visited. They are the ones responsible for the legislation that would bind the hands of the logging industry and result in so many lost jobs. If he obeys his company's orders he will be doing what any loyal employee should do, and he can save some jobs in the process. What should he do?

SUGGESTION: Much of the ethical tension in environmental issues centers around the issue of jobs versus the environment: is it possible to conserve the environment while we save and/or create jobs? Focus on this issue, and watch for red herrings as was discussed in the text. Also, ask yourself whether or not a job is a "right" every person has *as a person*. The Greeks, for example, thought that work was demeaning, but since the so-called "Protestant work ethic" began to prevail in this country in the nineteenth century, work has seemed necessary for self-esteem, if not for sustenance. However, if a federal fund, say, could provide enough money to sustain people comfortably without the need to work, would the world be a worse place to live in than it is now when everyone expects to hold a job? This is a key issue in this debate.

E2. Blane Jackson is the CEO of MacDougal Baggot, one of British Columbia's largest forest-products firms. His company has been clear-cutting the forest that comprises 80% of the land in that area for many years, and has recently expanded its cutting operation into an area near the village of Kyuquot on Northern Vancouver Island. The 249-mile-long island is being logged faster than any other part of British Columbia. Of its eighty-nine largest watersheds, only six remain uncut. Blane's company plans to begin operations in one of those areas next month, but there have been a number of protests by environmentalists and members of the Kyuquot tribe who reside in the area. Some of these people have met with Blane in his office and requested that he spare this area, a pristine wilderness on which the native people depend for their livelihood—chiefly hunting and fishing.

A committee appointed by the provincial government to study old-growth forests across the province has recommended that logging in those areas be suspended for two years. Blane is not bound by that recommendation, nor by the demands and requests of the people who have met with him. Furthermore, two years of delays will cost his company thousands of dollars, since the equipment is nearby and roads have already been cut to the logging areas. Such costs will almost certainly result in layoffs and increased costs to his customers, which will hurt his competitive edge. What should Blane do?

E3. Judge Leslie Bright is hearing an appeal in the Reserve Mining case involving a Minnesota taconite mining company that has been permitted for years to dump 67,000 tons of taconite tailings daily into Lake Superior. The Minnesota Pollution Control Agency, the Environmental Protection Agency of the federal government, and the U.S. Justice Department have insisted that the company cease its operations because the tailings comprise a health hazard to the residents of the area, who depend on the lake for their water supply. Also, they contend, the plant in Silver Bay, Minnesota, discharges particles into the air that can cause asbestosis, mesothelioma, and various forms of cancer.

Reserve contends that the evidence that the plant's activities pose a health threat is not compelling and cites evidence from Dr. Arnold Brown that "with respect to both air and water, the levels of fibers [in the discharge] is not readily susceptible of measurement," and cannot be shown, therefore, to be dangerous. Because a danger cannot be shown to exist, their lawyers contend, the plant should not be closed. Such a move would cause considerable economic distress in the area, since Reserve Mining employs 80% of Silver Bay's 3000 inhabitants. What should Judge Bright do?

E4. On March 28, 1979, Fred Dwyer, a maintenance engineer at Three Mile Island nuclear power station near Harrisburg, Pennsylvania, was shaken by an alarming series of events. At 4:00 A.M. a minor device in the reactor cooling system malfunctioned causing a series of valves to close, the main pumps to stop, and the power-generating turbine to shut down. Fred checked his gauges and noted that the heat in the reactor was rising rapidly. Apparently an auxiliary pump was supposed to start automatically, but someone had inadvertently left the valve shut and water could not enter the reactor to cool it down.

In a matter of moments, a safety valve opened because of increasing temperatures in the reactor, but the valve failed to shut down. As a result, steam was discharged into a drainage tank, and the reactor became so hot it shut down automatically. Only eight seconds had passed, but Fred was shaking and his heart was pounding in his chest. Lights and alarms were going off everywhere. Fred and his fellow engineers were convinced that the water pressure within the reactor was continuing to build so they shut down the pumps. The temperature in the reactor rose even higher.

As events became clearer later on, Fred realized that four operator errors had occurred along with two mechanical failures. Though they had come within an hour of a core meltdown that would have resulted in the death of thousands of area residents for whom evacuation plans were hopelessly inadequate, disaster was avoided by a series of steps Fred and his fellow engineers had taken subsequent to the events described above. Nevertheless, his confidence in the safety of nuclear plants was completely shaken.

As a result of this experience, Fred moved his wife and two small children to central Iowa and took a job with an electronics firm for $4,500 less in salary. He subsequently published several articles pointing out the dangers of nuclear power and the desirability of alternative sources of energy. Did he do the right thing? [HINT: The ethically right thing is not the same thing as what was right *for Fred*, which is to say, what made Fred feel good. Recall that the ethical perspective requires neutrality. The key issue here is this: what should anyone in Fred's place do?]

E5. Ralph Griffin is the CEO of a paper mill in northern Minnesota. He has been reading a great deal lately about acid rain and the depletion of the ozone layer, and since his company has operated for years without scrubbers on its smokestacks he knows that he is contributing to the problem. Scrubbers are very expensive and while their cost could be passed along to his customers, it would take years to pay for the new equipment and in the meantime his company would lose its competitive edge in the paper industry. This is especially true since none of the other companies in the area use scrubbers: they are not required by law, thanks to delays in clean-air legislation in Washington. Ralph has a deep love for the area where he has lived his entire life and he wants to make sure his grandchildren can enjoy the region for years to come. What should he do?

E6. In 1978 it was discovered that chemicals buried since the early 1940s in an abandoned section of the Niagara Falls area called Love Canal were seeping into the drinking water in an area of town where a new school and a fairly large residential complex had been completed a few years earlier. Several adults showed signs of incipient liver damage; young women in certain areas close to the canal experienced three times the normal rate of miscarriages; and the area had three and a half times the normal incidence of birth defects.

Hooker Chemical and Plastics Corporation admitted to burying the chemicals, but insisted that the burial was in strict accordance with regulations on the books at that time. In addition, they had warned the city of Niagara Falls not to build a school on that site, since the construction could damage the integrity of the clay bed in which the chemicals were buried. They had even received a signed statement from the city exempting the company from any responsibility in the event that injury or death to persons or damage to property arose from the construction of a school and a residential complex in that area.

Some argue that Hooker Chemical should bear the cost of cleaning up the area—estimated to run around $250 million. Still others argue that we should all pay the cost because we all use chemical products daily, many of which are produced by Hooker Chemical at its Niagara plant or elsewhere. A federal "Superfund" exists for the purpose of cleaning up toxic waste such as that buried in Love Canal. Hooker Chemical Company argues that the city of Niagara Falls should pay the cost since they knew the danger going in and went ahead and built a school on that site anyway. What do *you* think?

NOTES

INTRODUCTION

1. Karl Popper. *The Logic of Scientific Discovery.* New York: Harper and Row, 1968, p. 44.
2. Brand Blanshard. *Four Reasonable Men.* Middletown, CT: Wesleyan University Press, 1984, p. 247.

CHAPTER ONE

1. Philip Davis and Reuben Hersh. *Descartes' Dream.* Boston: Houghton Mifflin Co., 1986, p. 207.
2. Ibid., p. 213.
3. N. L. Gifford. *When In Rome.* New York: State University Press, 1983, p. 28.
4. Ibid., p. 77.
5. Giorgio Abetti. *The History of Astronomy* (tr. Betty Abetti). London: Abelard Schuman, 1952, p. 75.
6. Karl Popper. *Conjectures and Refutations.* New York: Harper and Row, 1965, p. 25.
7. Raphael Sealey. *A History of the Greek City-States.* California: University of California Press, 1976, p. 29.
8. Malcolm Todd. *Everyday Life of the Barbarians.* Dorset Press, 1972, p. 5.
9. Raphael Sealey. op. cit., p. 253.
10. Michael Polanyi. *Personal Knowledge.* Chicago: University of Chicago Press, 1962, p. 138.
11. Ibid.
12. Ibid., p. 4.
13. Ibid., p. 138.
14. *Louis de Broglie und die Physiker.* Quoted by Polanyi, op. cit., p. 148, note 1.

15. Abetti, op. cit., p. 72.
16. Ibid., p. 120.
17. Gordon Allport. *The Nature of Prejudice.* Boston: Beacon Press, 1954, p. 7.
18. Plutarch. *Lives of the Noble Grecians and Romans.* (tr. John Druden) New York: Modern Library, p. 62.

CHAPTER TWO

1. Immanuel Kant. *Lectures on Ethics.* New York: Harper and Row, p. 121.
2. Thomas Aquinas. *Summa Theologica.* 2a-2ac, *lxiv* 2 and 3.
3. Kant, op. cit., p. 197.
4. Eliseo Vivas. *The Moral Life and The Ethical Life.* Chicago: The University of Chicago Press, 1950, pp. 328–329.
5. Onora O'Neill. "Between Consenting Adults," *Philosophy and Public Affairs.* Vol. 14, #3. Italics in the original. Reprinted in Bayles and Henley. *Right Conduct: Theories and Applications.* New York: Random House, 1989, pp. 81–90.
6. One of the most interesting rule utilitarians writing today is the English philosopher R. M. Hare, whose version of utilitarianism arises from his adoption of a Kantian view and centers around what he calls "universalization"—an adaptation of Kant's categorical imperative that requires us to critically test moral principles by asking what would happen if *everyone* were to act as we propose to act in a given situation. Hare is convinced that his position avoids the shortcomings attributed to many versions of utilitarianism of "riding roughshod" over reciprocal human rights—which Hare also considers central to ethics. The view I am defending here simply makes explicit that concern for rights and stresses both rights and fairness as necessary conditions for ethical behavior. (Cf. R. M. Hare. *Moral Reasoning.* Oxford: Oxford University Press, 1981.)
7. R. M. Hare. *Moral Reasoning.* Oxford: Oxford University Press, 1981, p. 39.
8. James Hillman. *Re-Visioning Psychology.* New York: Harper and Row, 1975, p. 182.
9. John Rawls. *A Theory of Justice.* Cambridge: Harvard University Press, 1971, p. 140.
10. Hare. op. cit., p. 92.

CHAPTER THREE

1. David Kelly. *The Art of Reasoning.* New York: W. W. Norton, Inc., 1988, pp. 96–97.

CHAPTER FOUR

1. Ronald Dworkin. "Lord Devlin and the Enforcement of Morals." Reprinted in Wasserstrom. *Morality and the Law.* Belmont, CA: Wadsworth Publishing Co., 1971, pp. 63–64.
2. Gordon Allport. *The Nature of Prejudice.* Boston: Beacon Press, 1954.
3. Chaim Perelman and L. Obrechts-Tyteca. *The New Rhetoric.* Notre Dame: University of Notre Dame Press, 1969, pp. 31–35.

CHAPTER FIVE

1. O'Neill. op. cit. Italics are in the original.

GLOSSARY OF KEY TERMS USED IN THIS TEXT

ARGUMENT

As this term is used in this text, it refers to a series of statements that are connected by a logical relation called entailment. One of the statements is called the conclusion of the argument and the other statements (one or more) are called reasons or premises. The term contrasts with exposition which is a series of disconnected statements that do not support a conclusion (see Chapter Three).

CLAIM

Claims are either relative to the speaker or the speaker's culture, or they are nonrelative. A nonrelative claim professes to be about our shared world and may be true or false: It is open to verification or falsification by persons other than the speaker himself or herself. Some nonrelative claims are stronger than others in that the evidence in support of them is more likely to be true. The argument in this book seeks to support the view that ethics can involve nonrelative claims that are as strong or as weak as their rational support.

JUSTIFICATION

A process of rational argumentation by which claims are supported. This term usually refers to ethical judgments that purport to be true, that is to ethical claims. The term contrasts with rationalization which is an attempt to find good reasons to support positions that one holds for bad reasons—that is, personal or emotional commitments one is reluctant to abandon. (For both of these terms, as well as a discussion of good reasons, see Chapter Four.)

OBJECTIVISM (ALSO NONRELATIVISM)

This term contrasts with subjectivism or relativism (see below) and refers to the neutrality of claims, that is their lack of dependence upon the speaker or writer. Objectivism, that is, the doctrine, has reference to the thesis that claims are *objective*, that is, capable of independent verification. I follow Karl Popper (who follows Immanuel Kant) in insisting that knowledge claims (including ethical claims) are "objective [when they are] *justifiable*, independently of anybody's whim: a justification [in turn] is 'objective' if in principle it can be tested and understood by anybody... the *objectivity* of scientific statements [for example] lies in the fact that they can be *intersubjectively tested*." (Karl Popper: THE LOGIC OF SCIENTIFIC DISCOVERY, op. cit. p. 44) To the extent to which a claim is objective it is not subjective and *visa versa*.

RATIONALIZATION

See Justification above. Rationalization is the process of finding reasons *after the fact* for conclusions we hold for personal reasons (that is, reasons that have no universal appeal) and are reluctant to abandon.

RELATIVISM (SEE SUBJECTIVISM)

Refers to the relationship of beliefs to the one stating the beliefs. Beliefs are said to be relative to the speaker (in the case of subjectivism) or to the speaker's culture (in the case of cultural relativism). From a systematic point of view, both forms of relativism pose the same difficulties for one who seeks to defend objectivism, or the view that ethical judgments, for example, are not mere beliefs and are not simply relative to persons or cultures.

SUBJECTIVISM (SEE RELATIVISM)

One form of relativism in which claims merely reflect the personally held beliefs or opinions of the speaker.

INDEX

A

Act utilitarianism, 43, 44
Allport, Gordon, 26, 92
Apartheid, *xvii* ff.
Appeal to authority, 80 ff., 104
Appeal to emotion, 81 ff., 84
Aquinas, St. Thomas, 37
Aristotle, 11, 23, 31 ff., 34, 44
Argument, 49, 63
  Chapter Three. Argument chains, 72
  Argument webs, 72
  Argument evaluation, 70 ff.
  Argument support, 25
Assumptions, 17, 75, 83, 103. (*See also* Suppressed premises)
Authoritarianism, 29
Autonomy, 40. (*See also* Self-determination)

B

Bayles, Michael, 108, 110
Bentham, Jeremy, 43, 48. (*See also* Act utilitarianism)
Bias, 6, 8, 13, 20 ff., 28, 29, 95, 99
Bifurcation, 80, 85 ff., 103
Blanshard, Brand, *xiv*
Brahe, Tycho, 11
Bruno, Giordano, 11

C

Capital punishment, 48
Character, 32 ff. (*See also* Virtue)
Claims, *xi*, 1 ff., 10, 15
Coersion, 40, 41, 108 ff., 111, 113
Community, 32, 33, 51
Consent, 108
Consequences of actions, 44, 50 ff.
Copernicus, 10 ff., 21, 23
Cost/benefit, 45, 46. (*See also* Act utilitarianism)
Counter-examples, 70
Critical rationalism, 13, 29, 86
Cross-cultural judgments, 26, 28, 96
Cultural relativism, *xvii*, 4, 20 ff., 26, 28, 96

D

deBroglie, Louis, 23
Discrimination, 43
Dostoevsky, Fyodor, 38
Duties to self, 57, 118
Dworkin, Ronald, 91

E

Einstein, Albert, 23
Enlightened self-interest, 51

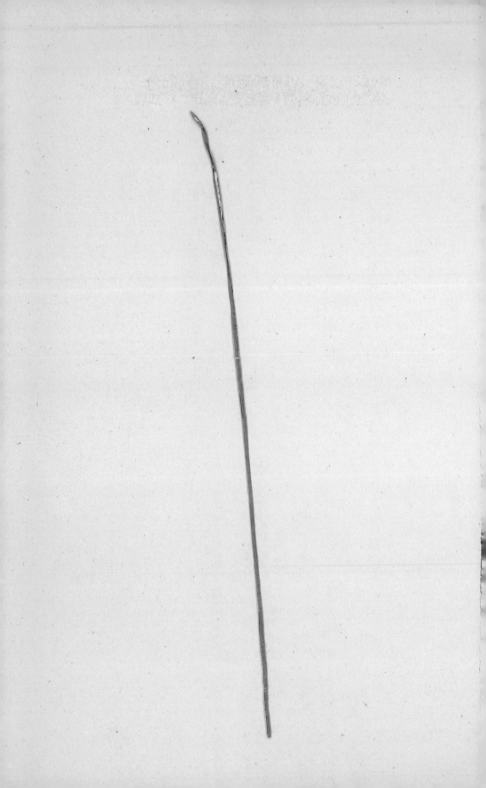